Major Mesozoic exposures of rocks in which dinosaurs might be found.

THE GREAT DINOSAURS

THE GREAT DINOSAURS

A Story of the Giants' Evolution

Prof. Zdeněk V. Špinar
Dr. Philip J. Currie
Illustrated by Jan Sovak

CAXTON EDITIONS

Half-title ~ *Procompsognathus triassicus*
Title page ~ *Parasaurolophus walkeri*

1. *Tyrannosaurus rex*
2. *Baryonyx walkeri*
3. *Carnotaurus sastrei*
4. *Ceratosaurus nasicornis*
5. *Dilophosaurus wetherilli*
6. *Alioramus remotus*
7. *Struthiomimus altus*
8. *Deinonychus antirrhopus*
9. *Oviraptor philoceratops*
10. *Ornitholestes hermanni*
11. *Compsognathus longipes*

Designed and produced by Aventinum Publishing House, Prague, Czech Republic
This edition published 2000 by CAXTON EDITIONS, an imprint of
The Caxton Publishing Group, 20 Bloomsbury Street, London WC1B 3JH

Copyright © 1994 AVENTINUM NAKLADATELSTVÍ, s. r. o.

Text by Prof. Zdeněk V. Špinar and Dr. Philip J. Currie
Translated by Slavoš Kadečka
Illustrations by Jan Sovak
Interior design by Ken Uyeda/DINOinc and Pavel Gaudore

ISBN 1-84067-276-5
Printed in the Czech Republic by Polygrafia, a.s., Prague
3/99/79/51-04

Dinosaurs are probably now, more than ever, the best known group of extinct animals. But what has prompted this sudden resurgence of public interest in these ancient reptiles?

It is true that the enormous dimensions of extinct dinosaurs have fascinated us since time immemorial. However, recent research undertaken by a few scientists has revealed some exciting new information about dinosaurs and intensified the attention of specialists working in this field throughout the world. Likewise, recently, the palaeontologists have made some surprising discoveries. For exemple, they have established that most dinosaurs were warm-blooded, that even the largest and heaviest of them did not live in water permanently, as most scientists had previously assumed, and that our contemporary birds actually developed from the theropod dinosaurs in the course of the middle Mesozoic formation – the Jurassic. Thus the dinosaurs have rapidly become the focus of intensive attention not only of the palaeontologists, but also of the general public.

Naturally this increasingly detailed study of dinosaurs has given rise to a broad range of questions which this book sets out to answer.

Nowadays an enormous number of publications and big picture atlases about dinosaurs are issued all over the world. Many of these just present the same facts, slightly modified, and, unfortunately, their information is often erroneous and outdated. For this reason we have tried to collect the latest results of dinosaur research to present to our readers.

The introductory chapters include an overview of the discovery and the study of dinosaurs, as well as some key information on their anatomy, their ability to adapt and other reasons for the great success of these bizarre reptiles. The dinosaurs are grouped according to the geological periods in which they occurred. In order to clarify the range of problems associated with the origin of new species, their proliferation and phylogenesis, these chapters also provide detailed coverage of the palaeobiogeography and the climatic conditions which exercised enormous influence on the origin of new species of dinosaurs.

The chapter on the oldest period of the Mesozoic – the Triassic – is concerned with the origin of the whole dinosaur group, their diversification and some anatomical characteristics which contributed to their position of superiority over all the other species of animals which existed at the end of the Triassic. Their worldwide proliferation, however, was also facilitated by the favourable palaeogeographic situation : all dry land was united then in a single super-continent – the Pangaea.

The individual groups of dinosaurs are described in terms of their geographic occurrence, their size, specific features of their body morphology, their behaviour and customs. The text is supplemented by numerous drawings and colour pictures showing the individual dinosaur species in their natural habitat. These pictures have been specifically created for this book by the renowned artist, Jan Sovak. There is also extensive information on the most famous discoveries of dinosaur skeletons and the dramatic circumstances which led up to these spectacular finds. The role played by chance, which

was, naturally, of great importance, was backed up by the painstaking, diligent work of many scientists and laymen.

The environment which formed during the Jurassic, however, engendered numerous other groups of animals – including the sauropods, cetiosaurs, diplodocids and brachiosaurs, the skeletal remains of which were discovered on new sites in South America, China, Australia and Antarctica. This section of the book also focuses on the theropods, another group which appeared in the Triassic and lived in the Jurassic, highlighting their anatomical features, area of occurrence and phylogenesis, as well as the primitive group of Thyreophora, which survived until the end of the Cretaceous.

In the last and longest period of the Mesozoic – the Cretaceous – when the Atlantic Ocean had already appeared and Gondwanaland had disintegrated, there were extremely favourable climatic conditions on Earth. During this period the development of the sauropods, theropods and numerous other groups of animals continued successfully. So why were the dinosaurs so successful in the Mesozoic and why did they die out? These fundamental questions have not yet been answered satisfactorily and represent an enigma for the palaeontologists of the 21st century.

The book also provides an update on current scientific expeditions in search of new dinosaur sites throughout the world, as well as on numerous new discoveries in Asia (China, Korea), South America, Africa and Australia. It concludes with a summary of the parks, museums and institutions in which one can see and study the skeletons of the dinosaurs, as well as the research programmes being undertaken by both laymen and scientists. Dinosaurs have actually survived to the present day in the rather unlikely form of birds, so there is a real possibility that they might even outlive the era of Man.

Zdeněk V. Špinar

Left ~ Almost a hundred million years ago, Carnotaurus may have used the horns over its eyes to warn a rival male from its territory.

TABLE OF CONTENTS

INTRODUCTION	10
History of Discovery of Dinosaurs	10
History of the Study of Dinosaurs	14
What Are the Dinosaurs?	16
Why Are Dinosaurs So Popular?	17
The Earliest Archosaurs ~ Ancestors of Dinosaurs	20
Crocodiles and Pterosaurs	21
THE OLDEST MESOZOIC FORMATION ~ THE TRIASSIC	24
Position of Continents	24
Climatic Conditions in the Triassic	25
Flora	25
Fauna	25
The Origin of Dinosaurs	26
The First Dinosaurs	28
Diversification of Dinosaurs	33
Theropoda	34
Sauropodomorpha	35
Dinosaurs at the End of the Triassic	37
THE MIDDLE OF THE MESOZOIC ~ THE JURASSIC PERIOD	38
Flora	38
Fauna	39
Dinosaurs in the Jurassic	42
Sauropoda	42
Cetiosauridae	48
Diplodocidae	48
Brachiosauridae	58
Camarasauridae	60
Theropoda	60
Ceratosauridae	63
Megalosauridae	67
Allosauridae	68
Coelurosauridae	72
Thyreophora	73
Stegosauria	73
THE CRETACEOUS ~ The Golden Age of Dinosaurs	78
Climatic Conditions	78
Flora	83
Fauna	84
Dinosaurs	86
SAURISCHIA	86
Sauropoda	86

TABLE OF CONTENTS

Predatory Dinosaurs ~ Theropoda	90
Carnosauria	90
Tyrannosauridae	91
Spinosauridae	93
Abelisauridae	96
Segnosauridae	96
Ornithomimidae	99
Deinocheiridae	99
Dromaeosauridae	100
Troodontidae	101
Other Theropods	103
ORNITHISCHIA	103
Ornithopoda	106
Hypsilophodontidae	106
Camptosauridae	108
Iguanodontidae	108
Hadrosauridae	109
Pachycephalosauridae	118
Stegosauria	124
Ankylosauria	125
Ceratopsia ~ the Horned Dinosaurs	127
Psittacosauridae	130
Protoceratopsidae	130
Ceratopsidae	134
WHY WERE DINOSAURS SO SUCCESSFUL?	141
Adaptation	142
Physiological Adaptation	142
Behavioural Adaptations	147
Eggs and Nests	149
Dinosaur Brains	152
The Environment	154
The Great Extinction	159
DINOSAUR EXPEDITIONS AROUND THE WORLD	162
WHERE CAN YOU SEE DINOSAURS?	170
Museums in which Dinosaurs Can be Seen	170
Dinosaur Parks	172
Volunteer Programmes	172
New Discoveries	173
Dinosaur Experts Active Today	174
CONCLUSION	174
INDEX	175

INTRODUCTION

In this book, the authors want to acquaint their readers with those extremely popular, mostly giant, extinct reptiles that were called dinosaurs by Richard Owen as early as 1841, and to show what they were, how they originated and how they lived.

The Dinosauria were highly successful during most of the Mesozoic, and ruled all continents for 160 million years. At present, dinosaurs are the focus of intensive research by scientists. The interest of laymen is demonstrated by the volume of popular and scientific publications, innumerable articles in newspapers and magazines, radio and television programmes, fictionalizations in comics, novels, movies and cartoons, a lucrative toy market, and visitation at the most popular of all museum displays - the dinosaur galleries.

The largest dinosaurs have captivated public attention not only by their enormous dimensions, but also by their sometimes bizarre adaptations, and their ways of life. Their popularity is heightened by new research and costly expeditions to the far corners of the world. Palaeontologists, anatomists, astronomers, chemists, ecologists, engineers, geologists, pathologists and physiologists are some of the scientists who have been attracted to do research on these fascinating animals. There are things being learned about dinosaurs today that we would not have thought possible even ten years ago. But discussion often leads to controversy, and in the true spirit of scientific method, theories are tested and new evidence is sought.

To better understand this extremely interesting group of animals, let us say first a few words about their discovery.

History of Discovery of Dinosaurs

The first dinosaur bone was described in 1677 by a museum custodian, Robert Plot, in his book "Natural History of Oxfordshire". Plot illustrated a fragment of a large bone that he considered, in accordance with the world outlook of that time, a fragment of a human giant. His drawing was good enough to show us that he actually had part of a bone of a big carnivorous dinosaur.

The first scientific discovery of dinosaurs, however, is attributed to Doctor Gideon Mantell and his wife, Mary Ann. Mantell was a medical practitioner in the town of Lewes (some 15 km south of London). Apart from medicine, he was keenly interested in the fossils found frequently in the Cretaceous sediments of southern England, and wanted to write a book about them. One spring day in 1822, Dr. Mantell visited one of his patients not far from the town. His wife, who often accompanied him on his rounds, went for a short walk while waiting for her husband. She noticed something shiny sticking out of a heap of gravel being used for road repairs, and recognized it as a large

The first unquestionable dinosaur bone was illustrated in 1677 by Robert Plot, who thought it was from a giant human. It was later described as *Scrotum humanum*, which in a sense is the first official dinosaur name.

fossil tooth. When her husband joined her, he knew immediately it was a tooth of an unknown herbivorous animal, but could not identify its species or order. In spite of that, he managed to put a drawing of the tooth made by his wife in his book on fossils, which appeared in 1822. Soon afterwards, Mantell learned that the road gravel had come from a quarry twelve kilometres from the town of Lewes. He was able to visit the quarry and find more teeth and numerous bone fragments. He also began an intensive search to identify the animal to which these remains belonged. He even sent the bones to Paris for examination by Baron Georges Cuvier, a leading palaeontologist and comparative anatomist of that time. At first Cuvier thought that the tooth belonged to a fossil rhinoceros, and identified some of the other fossils as the remnants of a hippopotamus. Mantell, however, was not content with these identifications and continued his search. He showed the tooth and the skeletal fragments to Dr. Buckland, professor of geology at the University in Oxford, and to other leading figures of contemporary science. However, he did not agree with their identifications either. Therefore he made comparisons with the enormous collection of fossilized and modern animals in the Hunterian Museum of the Royal College of Surgeons in London. There, he met a young man, Samuel Stutchbury, who was studying Central American lizards and immediately noticed the remarkable likeness between the fossil teeth and the teeth of certain lizards. Mantell was impressed by the comparison, classified his finds as extinct reptiles, and published his conclusions in "The Philosophical Transactions of the Royal Society of London" in 1825. He called the new animal *Iguanodon* (*Iguana* = lizard + *odon* = tooth). In this way the remains of unknown and unnamed group of reptiles have become a part of human consciousness.

Mary Ann Mantell found the tooth of an enormous fossil reptile in 1822. Her husband Gideon Mantell knew that the animal from which the tooth came was new to science, and gave it the name *Iguanodon*.

At about the same time that Gideon Mantell was trying to identify his fossils, William Buckland began taking an interest in a jaw bone with sabrelike teeth. This and other big fossil bones were found in Jurassic sediments near Stonesfield in Oxfordshire. Buckland published the first scientific description of a dinosaur in 1824, giving the carnivorous animal the scientific name of *Megalosaurus*. This name had been introduced in 1822 by the English doctor and geologist James Parkinson in his book "Outlines of Oryctology: an Introduction to the Study of Fossil Organic Remains", where he mentioned a fossil tooth that he referred to as *Megalosaurus*.

Mary Ann Mantell

The discovery of these giant fossilized bones showed that extraordinary big, unknown reptiles once lived in the world. These animals were christened by the famous English anatomist and palaeontologist Richard Owen (1804-1892), who in 1842 gave them the scientific name Dinosauria. He made up this name from the Greek words of *deinos* (= dreadful, terrible) and *sauros* (= reptile, lizard). Owen based dinosaurs on three imperfectly known types of terrestrial animals that were very different from modern reptiles. Initially Owen considered the dinosaurs as a single order. However, in 1887,

Gideon Mantell

Harry Govier Seeley used the structure of the hips to divide dinosaurs into two separate lineages, Saurischia and Ornithischia, a concept that is still recognized today.

The first thorough research of dinosaurs in North America was carried out by two enthusiastic, rival palaeontologists — Edward Drinker Cope and Othniel Charles Marsh. Cope (1840-1897) was a professor at the University of Pennsylvania who undertook intensive research on dinosaurs, other reptiles, fish, amphibians and mammals. Marsh (1831-1899) was the first professor of palaeontology at Yale University, but was financially backed by his uncle, who also founded Yale's Peabody Museum of Natural History. Both scientists were rich and could devote their time and energies to their research. These fervid palaeontologists were partisans of the theory of evolution, and knew personally all the contemporary naturalists of importance, including Darwin, Haeckel, Huxley, Owen and Kowalewski.

A famous era of dinosaur research in America is connected with the construction of the Union Pacific Railway. In the summer of 1877, Marsh received a letter from two workers informing him they had found bones of giant dimensions near a site where the railway tracks were being laid. They knew him as an enthusiastic geologist and man of means, and especially because of the latter wanted to make his acquaintance. It came to pass that the workers indeed had found a very rich dinosaur site. The Morrison Formation, named after the community of Morrison near Denver, has become one of the richest Upper Jurassic dinosaur sites. The rocks of this formation stretch from the Canadian border to New Mexico, and were deposited in a variety of environments suitable for dinosaurs to live in, and for the preservation of their bones as fossils. In some cases, the rivers carried the carcasses of dinosaurs from great distances, and deposited them on sandbars adjacent to the channels. These great bonebeds, the most famous of which is at Dinosaur National Monument in Utah, have produced thousands of skeletons and isolated bones of dinosaurs, and the animals that lived with the dinosaurs, such as fish, frogs, turtles, crocodiles, flying reptiles and mammals. For several years, men working for Marsh and Cope amassed tremendous collections of dinosaurs that were shipped back east for study and description by the archrivals. The sites are still productive, and bear names like Cope's Quarry, Marsh's Quarry, and Big Dinosaur Quarry. One such site, Bone Cabin, was discovered in 1898 by an expedition of the American Museum of Natural History in New York headed by a talented young palaeontologist, Henry Fairfield Osborn (1857-1935).

By the end of the 19th century, attention had shifted farther north to dinosaurs of the Late Cretaceous. The first specimens of *Tyrannosaurus* and *Triceratops* were excavated in Wyoming and Montana by American Museum of Natural History field parties,

E. D. Cope

A great rivalry developed in North America between O. C. Marsh (Yale University) and E. D. Cope (University of Pennsylvania) in the second half of the 19th century. Field parties working for these two men opened up the great dinosaur fossil sites of western North America. Cope and Marsh named and described many of the most famous dinosaurs, including *Allosaurus, Apatosaurus, Barosaurus, Camarasaurus, Camptosaurus, Ceratosaurus, Diplodocus, Monoclonius, Nodosaurus, Ornithomimus, Stegosaurus, Torosaurus* and *Triceratops*.

O. C. Marsh

usually led by Barnum Brown. In 1910, Brown set out in a barge to explore the badlands along the Red Deer River in Canada. He had remarkable success, and was soon competing with rival parties from the Geological Survey of Canada headed by one of Cope's collectors, Charles H. Sternberg. The Canadian Dinosaur Rush lasted for more than a decade, and hundreds of skeletons were shipped to institutions around the world. The most productive stretch of badlands, known as Dead Lodge Canyon, was established as Dinosaur Provincial Park in 1955, and in 1979 became the first palaeontological site on UNESCO's World Heritage List. More than 400 skeletons representing 35 species of dinosaurs have been collected there, making it one of the richest sites anywhere. In addition to the dinosaurs, more than 75 species of fish, frogs, salamanders, turtles, lizards, alligators, crocodiles, flying reptiles, birds and mammals have been identified.

Dinosaurs also attracted considerable attention in Europe. A great sensation was caused by the discovery in a Belgian coal mine of 39 skeletons of *Iguanodon*, the dinosaur whose tooth had been found by Mary Ann Mantell in England in 1822. These skeletons were found at Bernissart near the French border. Miners driving a gallery 322 m below ground level encountered great numbers of Lower Cretaceous bones in dark grey clays. They called Louis Dollo (1857-1931), a young palaeontologist from the Royal Museum in Brussels, who supervised the removal of the fossils. The mining engineers cut the clay into one cubic metre blocks, which they encased in solid shells of plaster to transport to the ground. The preparation and study of the material was done in the Museum. The number of fossils recovered from the mine exceeded all expectations, and included some 2,000 fishes of several orders, five crocodiles, five turtles, one salamander and an enormous quantity of fossil plants.

The occurrence of 39 *Iguanodon* skeletons at Bernissart naturally raised a number of questions. The remains of the animals were closely packed in a narrow but deep (34 m) fissure of clay. Originally, it was concluded that the Bernissart site used to be a narrow gulf into which rivers or the tide brought the corpses of *Iguanodon*. The corpses sank to the bottom, where they were covered with mud. Today it is known that the animals were living in a marsh, and that the skeletons were buried in the muds on at least three separate occasions.

Although never preserved, a horny beak encased the front of the jaws, and its shape can be seen in the bones that supported it. The complex dentition of multiple rows of teeth is well known, and was capable of crushing and chopping even tough fibrous plants. *Iguanodon* walked on its strong hind legs, and used its much weaker front limbs for the collection of food, possibly for defence, and periodically for extra support. When walking, the front part of the body was balanced by the tail.

C. H. Sternberg

C. H. Sternberg was one of E. D. Cope's collectors in the American west. In 1911, he went to work for the Geological Survey of Canada. Along with his three sons, he helped open up the rich fossil fields along the Red Deer River in Alberta. Specimens he collected can be found in the displays and collections of major museums and universities in North America and Europe.

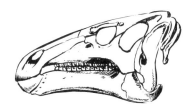

Many skulls, skeletons and footprints of *Iguanodon* have been found in Belgium, England, Germany and other countries, making it one of the best understood dinosaurs. The bones at the front of the mouth supported a horny beak that is never fossilized.

In Germany, it was Professor Friedrich von Huene (1875-1969) who became an excellent 20th century scholar in the field of dinosaurs. In 1921, he began studying the rich deposits of *Plateosaurus* bones from a quarry near Trössingen, Germany. Later he greatly increased our knowledge of the dinosaurs not only of Europe, but also of South America. He published numerous scientific papers, and finally summed up his extensive experience in the book "Paläontologie und Phylogenie der niederen Tetrapoden", published in 1956.

After the initial discovery of dinosaurs, large expeditions went to the desolate corners of the world, including Argentina, China, India, Mongolia and Tanzania, to seek the remains of dinosaurs. The most famous expedition was to China and Mongolia, where the Third Central Asiatic Expedition of the American Museum of Natural History set out in 1922 to discover if Asia was the birthplace of man. The motivation was provided by Henry Fairfield Osborn, who had predicted that many major groups of mammals must have originated in Asia. The fieldwork was directed by Roy Chapman Andrews, a biologist and explorer who had a flair for organizing and finding funding for major expeditions. Although the expeditions continued until 1930, they failed in their prime objective of finding early human remains. But they opened up what was still largely an unmapped region that up to that time had produced only a handful of fossils. In 1922, they discovered in Mongolia a fantastic site that they called the Flaming Cliffs, but which is now known as Bayn Dzak. The soft red sediments produced lots of dinosaur bones. And in the little bit of time they spent there in 1922, they picked up what they thought might be a bird egg. When they returned the following year, numerous nests of eggs were found, and there could be no doubt that they had been laid by dinosaurs. Dinosaur eggs caught the interest of the public, and made the expeditions famous worldwide. This was one of the last of the large scale dinosaur-hunting expeditions until money became available again in the 1970s. In spite of public and scientific interest in dinosaurs, research on these animals ground to a halt for more than half a century as funds were diverted into two World Wars and a Depression.

The relationships of animals are often understood better when displayed in a family tree. Dinosaurs are a branch high in the reptilian family tree. Their closest relatives were the flying reptiles (pterosaurs). Progressively more distant reptiles include crocodiles, lizards, and turtles.

History of the Study of Dinosaurs

As we have already mentioned, H. G. Seeley used pelvic structure to divide dinosaurs into the lizard-hipped (saurischian) and bird-hipped (ornithischian) forms. Over the years, an ever increasing number of palaeontologists were inclined to believe that both types of dinosaurs were no more closely related to each other than either was to crocodiles, pterosaurs and birds. Because of this, the name dinosaur lost its meaning for a time, and was used only informally, not scientifically.

A great change in the study of dinosaurs took place in the 1970s, when Drs. Robert Bakker, Peter Dodson, Jim Farlow, Peter Galton, John Ostrom, Dale Russell and others started to publish new theories to explain the success and extinction of dinosaurs. Whereas earlier studies were often done by geologists and focused on the naming and description of new and unusual forms, the new generation of dinosaur palaeontologists were biologists who were more interested in looking at dinosaurs as living animals.

Work by Bakker and Galton showed that both lineages of dinosaurs had a common ancestor that could be defined as a dinosaur. Therefore, it is correct to use the name Dinosauria.

Research suggests that dinosaurs, like birds and mammals, may have been warm-blooded animals, capable of maintaining their body temperatures at constant levels. Although the idea that birds were the direct descendents of dinosaurs had been proposed as early as 1870 by Thomas Huxley, it was not until almost a century later that the idea became more widely accepted, thanks to the work of John Ostrom at Yale University. On the basis of their own and Ostrom's studies, Bakker and Galton went so far as to suggest dinosaurs should be removed from the Reptilia, and with birds should be considered as a separate group, the Dinosauria. Today, most palaeontologists accept this concept. The evidence for these and other theories will be discussed later in the book.

Although not everyone accepts the idea that dinosaurs were warm-blooded, the majority of palaeontologists feel the evidence is strong enough to show that some, if not all, dinosaurs were. The Dinosauria, which include the saurischian and ornithischian lineages of Seeley plus birds (Aves), clearly can no longer be considered as reptiles in the traditional sense. The recognition in the 1970s that dinosaurs are more comparable in many ways to mammals and birds than to turtles, lizards, snakes and crocodiles signalled the beginning of a revolution in our thinking about one of the most successful land animals that the world has ever known. A resurgence in interest amongst researchers has led to a steady increase in our knowledge base since that revolution of thought. And this renaissance has been reflected by public interest, which is now at an all-time high. Humans, after all, like success stories. And with more than 8,000 species of feathered dinosaurs flying around the world today, we can no longer consider dinosaurs as failures.

Birds are believed to be the direct descendants of dinosaurs, and therefore most palaeontologists consider them as part of the Dinosauria. Crocodiles were more distant relatives that have survived until the present day. A number of other diverse groups of animals that are often referred to as thecodonts are part of a larger branch called the Archosauria, which includes crocodiles, pterosaurs, dinosaurs and birds.

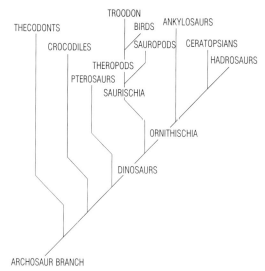

What Are the Dinosaurs?

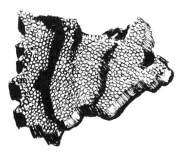

Skin impressions are known for some species of theropods, sauropods, hadrosaurs, ceratopsians, ankylosaurs and stegosaurs. Most dinosaurs had thick skin that was covered with small bumps or tubercles, and were not the big scaly monsters as they are often portrayed in movies.

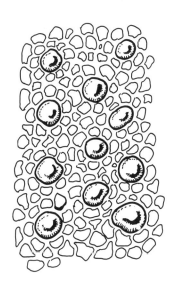

The scales of ankylosaurs are actually bony plates that form in the skin. In forms like *Edmontonia*, large plates are surrounded by small ones.

Dinosaurs are diapsid reptiles of varied sizes, appearances and ways of life. Initially, they were agile, fast moving carnivorous animals, capable of running on their hind legs when in a hurry. Much later forms became permanent quadrupeds as they became too large to support their weight on their hind limbs alone. All of these were herbivorous. Dinosaurs included the largest animals that ever lived on land. Weight estimates for some of the giant sauropods exceed 80 tonnes, and recent finds suggest that some species grew to more than 50 metres in length. Nevertheless, not all dinosaurs were big, and some were bigger as adults than a chicken.

Fossilized skin impressions have been found with the skeletons of most major types of large dinosaurs, and suggest that most dinosaurs had a thick, but essentially naked skin. Some dinosaurs, such as ankylosaurs and some sauropods, had thick plates of bone in their skin. In comparison with overall body size, the majority of dinosaurs had relatively small skulls, reflecting the small sizes of the brains and the lack of teeth suitable for chewing their food. Yet these generalities cannot be applied universally to dinosaurs. Ceratopsians (horned dinosaurs) had batteries of teeth for chopping up tough plants, and if you include the elaborate crests at the back of their skulls, these dinosaurs hold the record for the largest skulls of any land animal. Not all dinosaurs had small brains either. For example, the brain of the small carnivore *Troodon* is six times the size of the brain of a crocodile with the same body weight, and this suggests it was as intelligent as any of the mammals or birds that lived at the same time.

Dinosaur teeth, like those of crocodiles and the earliest birds, were set in sockets. The vertebrae were amphicoelous, opisthocoelous, platycoelous or procoelous and were often hollow. The number of neck vertebrae varied between 7 and 15, the number of dorsal ones between 10 and 19, the number of sacrals between 3 and 11, and there were as many as 70 tail vertebrae. The ribs had two heads, and the front limbs were usually shorter than the hind legs.

The pelvis consisted of three bones (ilium, pubis and ischium), all of which participated in the formation of the hip joint for the leg. The hip joint is not a solid socket as it is in crocodiles and most other reptiles more primitive than dinosaurs, but has a large opening on the inside. Pelvic structure has traditionally been important in the classification of dinosaurs. In lizard-hipped (saurischian) dinosaurs, the pubis generally projects down and forward, and the ischium down and backward. The orientations of the ilium and ischium are similar in bird-hipped (ornithischian) dinosaurs, but the pubis has both forward and backward extensions. Although the hips of bird-hipped dinosaurs superficially resemble those of birds, they are different in details, and the hip structure of birds actually evolved from the lizard-hipped dinosaurs.

Some of the most important characteristics used to define the Dinosauria are found in the hind limb. This is because dinosaurs were more efficient walkers than more primitive cousins like thecodonts, crocodiles and pterosaurs (flying reptiles). The upper leg bone (femur) has a ball-like head that fits into the hip socket and brings the leg under the body. Of the two bones in the lower part of the leg, the outer one (fibula) is much thinner than the inner one (tibia). One of the ankle bones (astragalus) is firmly attached to the tibia, and has a long extension in front of the shin to strengthen the contact.

Saurischian and ornithischian dinosaurs have been found in the 225 million year old rocks of Argentina, and both lineages speedily propagated and diversified to become the dominant animals by the end of the Triassic. And dinosaurs persevered as the ruling animals until the end of the Mesozoic, some 160 million years later.

Why Are Dinosaurs So Popular?

As we have already seen, dinosaurs have only been known scientifically since 1824. Their big bones had been found from time to time before that, but people either did not pay any attention to these finds, or they considered them as the remains of fairy tale dragons in accordance with their world outlook at that time. It was not until the 19th century when a rational outlook of the world and the laws of nature developed, that some scientists concluded that the giant bones belonged to entirely unknown animals whose size exceeded anything human fantasy had ever imagined. People were astounded by the enormous dimensions of skeletons that were being excavated by the end of the 19th century. Children, because of their interest in superlatives, were excited by the pictures of these huge animals that had actually been alive, and saw in them a personification of the monsters of their fantasies.

In recent years, there has been a complete transformation of our knowledge of the way dinosaurs looked, lived and interacted, and we are much closer to understanding why they were so successful for so long. Rather than removing the mystique, dinosaurs have become more fascinating as we uncover the complexities of their world. Think of it, they were animals that outcompeted mammals for 160 million years. They may have been warm-blooded, they cared for their young, they colonized the polar regions, they migrated in huge herds, and, if you accept that birds are feathered dinosaurs, they did not die out at the end of the Cretaceous period. It is no wonder that dinosaurs are attracting ever more public attention, and that they are the object of interest of journalists, publishers, film-makers, and television teams. But more than that, they have become a cultural phenomenon. They have become the stars of art shows, cartoons, comic strips, science fiction books and movies. The likenesses of dinosaurs are found on advertisements, clothing, furniture, trading cards, wallpaper, dishes, and hundreds of other products. It

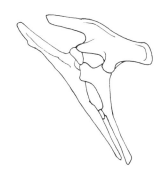

Bird hips

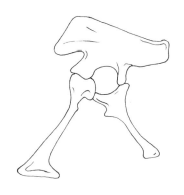

Lizard hips

Like other tetrapods, dinosaurs have three hip bones on each side. All three contribute to the socket for the upper leg bone, but the median wall of the socket is pierced by a hole. The pubis of an ornithischian (bird-hipped) dinosaur has two processes, one of which extends backwards underneath the ischium. In saurischian (lizard-hipped) dinosaurs, the pubis usually faces forward.

Following page ~ Archaeopteryx, the earliest known bird, and Compsognathus, one of the smallest dinosaurs, attempt to scare each other away from a tasty seafood supper (Aspidorhynchus). Birds are the direct descendants of small, carnivorous dinosaurs like Compsognathus.

is predicted that US$ 500,000,000.00 will be spent on dinosaur toys and other products following the success of the movie "Jurassic Park".

Dinosaurs have not died out completely. Their feathered descendants are living in enormous numbers all over the Earth, and in numbers of species they are still more successful than mammals. Few people realize when relishing an egg for breakfast, or a roast turkey, goose, duck or chicken at a festive dinner, that they are actually enjoying

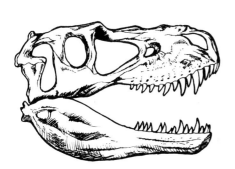

the taste of a somewhat changed, but well adapted dinosaur. And although the largest dinosaurs died out at the end of the Cretaceous 65 million years ago, one of the great mysteries of the world, they have their place in our thoughts, and in that sense will always be successful.

The Earliest Archosaurs ~ Ancestors of Dinosaurs

Dinosaurs, birds, crocodiles, pterosaurs and a number of other animals are collectively known as the Archosauria. Archosaurs share a common ancestor with lizards and snakes, and are therefore classified with them as the Diapsida. Diapsids have two openings in the temporal region behind the eye, although the bars of bone that surround these openings can be lost in advanced forms like snakes and birds.

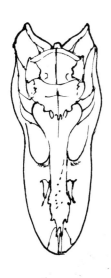

Archosaurs are easy to distinguish from more primitive reptiles because of numerous special adaptations. For example, they have an extra opening, the antorbital window, in the skull between the eye and the external nostril. There is also an opening in the side of the lower jaw. The teeth have relatively long roots and are set in sockets. At the back of the skull, the supratemporal bone has been lost, and the pineal opening in the top of the skull is rarely developed. The backbone consists of amphicoelous or platycoelous vertebrae. The ribs are two headed. There are well developed abdominal ribs, thin bony elements protecting the soft underside of the abdomen between the chest and the hips. The front limbs are usually shorter and more gracile than the hind limbs. The most primitive archosaurs are often referred to as thecodonts. These small but phylogenetically very important animals include the ancestors of dinosaurs, crocodiles and pterosaurs.

Dinosaurs are diapsids. That is, they have two holes on each side of the skull behind the eye. The key-hole shaped opening closest to the back of the skull is called the lateral temporal opening. The upper temporal opening is on top of the skull. Lizards, snakes and crocodiles are living examples of the Diapsida.

Thecodonts, which first appeared at the end of the Permian, included both carnivorous and herbivorous species. They were successful during the Triassic, and included such diverse forms as the armoured aetosaurs and the crocodile-like phytosaurs. By the end of the period, they had been replaced by dinosaurs.

Crocodiles and Pterosaurs

During the Triassic, dinosaurs, crocodiles and pterosaurs arose independently from thecodonts. Crocodiles are the least specialized of the three groups in appearance, and their essential characters have changed little since the Mesozoic. The skulls are massive, and the antorbital opening between the eye and external nostril is either reduced in size or closed completely. There is a secondary palate, a bony plate in the roof of the mouth that directs air from the nostrils directly into the throat. The quadrate, a bone at the back of the skull that articulates with the lower jaw, has very complex relationships with the bones around it. Several skull bones have been lost. Although modern crocodiles are characterized by their sprawling limbs, the earliest forms were gracile animals that ran on their hind limbs and looked similar to some of the earliest dinosaurs. By adopting an aquatic lifestyle in the Jurassic, they escaped competition with dinosaurs.

Aetosaurs like *Stagonolepis* (above) were armoured archosaurs from the Triassic Period. Although phytosaurs (*Parasuchus*, below) were archosaurs that looked like crocodiles, they are not closely related. The nostrils of phytosaurs have shifted far back on the skull and were located on top of a mound of bone.

Quetzalcoatlus, the largest known pterosaur, commanded the attention of its smaller dinosaurian relatives. Dromaeosaurs would have kept their distance until the gigantic glider left the ceratopsian it was scavenging.

21

The flying reptiles, or pterosaurs, first appeared in Late Triassic times. By the time pterosaurs appeared, they were already highly adapted for flying, and this makes it difficult to determine their precise ancestry. A small bipedal reptile from Scotland, *Scleromochlus*, is considered by some to be a good ancestral form for both pterosaurs and dinosaurs. This 20 cm long animal has a relatively large head, a strap-shaped shoulder blade, and a backbone that is divided into distinct regions. The legs are long, and the ankle bones are similar to those of pterosaurs. Friedrich von Huene even speculated that *Scleromochlus* may have lived in trees and had gliding membranes.

The fifth (outer) toe of the foot is still well developed in the earliest pterosaurs, whereas this toe is reduced in size in the most advanced thecodonts and dinosaurs. This suggests that pterosaurs evolved from thecodonts earlier than dinosaurs did, but other specializations show that they are closer to dinosaurs than crocodiles are.

Pterosaurs are most easily characterized by their wings, although they have specialized features throughout their bodies. The wing is supported by the fourth finger of their hand, which is greatly elongated. The wing membrane stretched from the end of the finger to the base of the legs in most forms. Contrary to popular belief, most pterosaurs were active fliers like birds and bats, but some were specialized for gliding. They reached their peak of success during the Jurassic period, and declined in numbers and diversity throughout the Cretaceous, probably because of competition with birds. The last pterosaurs escaped this competition by becoming the largest gliding animals ever known. The wingspan of *Quetzalcoatlus* of North America is estimated to have been more than 12 m.

Pterosaurs, or flying reptiles, were the first cousins of dinosaurs. They are characterized by their unique membraneous wings, which are supported by a single finger (the fourth finger). The other three fingers functioned normally. The wing membrane was stiffened by thin rods of cartilage or some other tough material.

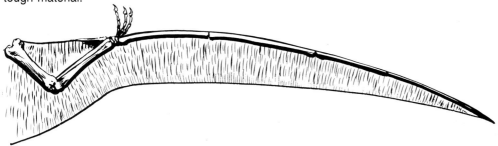

Opposite page ~ A pair of miniature Scleromochlus would have found little comfort in the knowledge that their descendants might include two successful groups, the dinosaurs and pterosaurs. More than 200 million years ago in ancient Scotland, their major concern was finding enough food to survive.

THE OLDEST MESOZOIC FORMATION
~ THE TRIASSIC

Dinosaurs originated in the period that geologists call the Triassic, covering about the first forty million years of the Mesozoic. The world was entirely different from that which we know now, with different flora and fauna. The continents were united at that time in a single enormous supercontinent known as Pangaea. Neither the lower nor the upper boundaries of the Triassic are sharply defined, and are difficult to determine in some areas.

Position of Continents

At the end of the Palaeozoic, in the Permian, the southern part of Pangaea was still covered with ice. As the ice cover receded, the level of the world oceans rose, flooding the continental margins and increasing the size of epicontinental seas. On Pangaea, much of the area between the tropics and the southern polar circle was arid. The monsoonal air flow regime, in which the winds brought moisture from the seas to the continent, prevailed in summer at higher latitudes. But the winds blew in the opposite direction in winter. Adequate moisture all year round was available only in polar regions. The breakup of Pangaea had not started yet, although the increased accumulation of continental sediments with evaporites indicates the incipient drop in the equatorial zone.

In Europe, we distinguish two trends of development of Triassic sedimentation: the German and the Alpine. Both were named after the areas in which they were observed and described for the first time. The differences in the development of these types of Triassic sediments are considerable. In its German development, the Triassic consists of continental, oceanic, lagoonal and brackish sediments. The strata attain thicknesses of several hundred metres, and it is possible to see how the sediments settled in areas alternately above sea level and flooded by the sea. When above water, the low, flat regions were richly vegetated. The Triassic sediments of Alpine development, on the other hand, settled in the seas. Mighty volumes of limestones and dolomites attained much greater thicknesses than the strata of the German development, because they were deposited in dropping basins.

The Tethys Sea, in which the sediments of the Alpine development settled, extended east-west in the area where the present-day Alps stand. The land north of Tethys was limited to the north by the Arctic sea.

Africa, South America, Australia, Antarctica and India were still united in a single supercontinent. Its gradual disintegration began before the Triassic ended, proceeding along north-south faults that divided the continent into western (Afro-American) and eastern (Indo-Australian) parts. Intensive volcanic activity is known to have occurred in South America, South Africa and in Siberia during the Triassic. But in other parts of the world, the Triassic was a relatively peaceful period tectonically.

During the Triassic, the continents were united in a huge continent known as Pangaea. Because all continents were connected, the first dinosaurs were free to move between all land masses.

Climatic Conditions in the Triassic

The climatic conditions in the Triassic were relatively stable and warm following widespread global transgression (overflow of the seas onto land). The expansion of shallow seas produced a generally warmer climate with tropical, subtropical and mild zones extending to relatively high geographic latitudes. Large inland regions were covered with deserts because no moisture-laden oceanic winds could reach them. A significant feature of the Triassic climatic zoning was the absence of the equatorial humid zone, and an arid zone extended from the tropics to the polar circle in the south.

At the end of the Triassic, the seas retreated (regressed) from the land, which resulted in climatic cooling. Although this trend was of short duration, it led to the restructuring of whole ecosystems, and the extinction of numerous groups of animals. After this, a long warm period set in again. Overall, the Triassic climate was so favourable that coal could even form in some areas. But in other, drier areas, sediments of conspicuous red and crimson colours were laid down, often with deposits of salt.

Flora

In the warm climates of the Triassic, plants thrived in the more humid regions. Gymnosperms, including *Araucaria* and *Ginkgo*, were widespread because they were well adapted for dry environments. Cycadophytes were widespread, either tree-shaped or barrel-shaped, with long leathery, most frequently pinnate leaves. In appearance they recall some tree-sized ferns or palms. Also, the Bennettitales (Cycadeoidales) were widespread in the form of richly forked bushes or trees. Rocks were covered with creeping ferns (Gleicheniaceae), and horsetails, although not as big as those of the Palaeozoic, grew in swamps and ponds. Coniferous trees, such as firs, cypresses, and yews had appeared.

Fauna

Life was rich in the seas, the most important position being occupied by cephalopods, especially ammonites. Also decapod crabs appeared for the first time in the Triassic. Fresh waters were richly enlivened by ray-finned (actinopterygian) fishes, which also penetrated salt waters during the Triassic.

Large amphibians, stegocephalians, thrived in the favourable climate of the Early Triassic. Their number included *Trematosaurus* - an amphibian feeding on marine fish. Most stegocephalians died out at the end of the Triassic. At the same time, the only known ancestor of modern frogs appeared: the skeleton of *Triadobatrachus massinoti* was found in Madagascar in 1938.

The Triassic was the period of enormous development of reptiles, which invaded both water and air from their land base. During the course of that period, these reptiles, who were highly sensitive to the changes of climate, even produced the archetypes of what was to become one of most important groups of vertebrates - the mammals.

Araucaria, the Norfolk Island Pine, is a beautiful coniferous tree whose relatives have been around since the Triassic. Tree trunks preserved in Petrified Forest National Park in the United States are from Triassic araucariacean trees.

Therapsids are the mammal-like reptiles that diversified greatly during the transition from the Permian to the Triassic. The mostly herbivorous types are referred to the Anomodontia, and the mostly carnivorous forms to the Theriodontia. The anomodontian mammal-like reptiles multiplied greatly, but generally stagnated in their evolution. The theriodontian mammal-like reptiles were far more progressive, and created a number of lineages in the Triassic in which it is already possible to distinguish mammalian characters. In the Late Triassic, most mammal-like reptiles disappeared. However, the first true mammals had already appeared. They do not appear to have been numerous, but were widespread. The first mammals were small animals, comparable in size to mice or sewer-rats, which lived concealed in the shade of the then intensively developing dinosaurs.

Thecodont archosaurs, which have already been introduced, were essentially Triassic animals, and reached their peak of diversity before the appearance of dinosaurs.

The Origin of Dinosaurs

The earliest known dinosaurs are from the Late Triassic of Argentina and Brazil, and lived about 228 million years ago. These dinosaurs were already diverse, and this suggests that they had first evolved sometime in the Middle Triassic. The probable ancestral thecodont family, the Ornithosuchidae, form the base of a branch on the family tree known as the Ornithosuchia. In addition to ornithosuchids, this branch includes *Lagosuchus* from Argentina, pterosaurs, dinosaurs and birds. *Lagosuchus* was a small (30 cm long), lightly-built animal from the middle Triassic. Its backbone was differentiated into various regions, and its hind legs are advanced like those of all dinosaurs. It is believed that the ancestor of all groups of dinosaurs would have looked very much like *Lagosuchus*. Unfortunately, the fossilized remains of these delicate animals are rare and not much is known about them. Theories are only as good as their evidence, and it is not surprising there are other opinions about the origin of dinosaurs. For example, Dr. Tony Thulborn of Australia feels that Triassic footprint evidence suggests that theropods, sauropodomorphs (prosauropods and sauropods) and ornithischians arose independently from bipedal ancestors over a period of as much as ten million years.

Eoraptor, the most primitive dinosaur presently known, was a relatively small animal from the Triassic of Argentina. Major evolutionary changes usually take place in small animals because they have shorter generations, and produce more young than their larger relatives.

As these animals became larger, the hind legs became substantially stronger to support most of the weight. The hips are loaded during such movement, and undergo remarkable structural changes. From a flat, primitive structure they developed into a strong triradiate girdle with a substantially thickened ilium, and elongate pubic and ischial bones to increase the length and improve the direction of action of the leg muscles. The adaptation to different modes of movement produced two types of pelvic girdles in lagosuchid descendants. As dinosaurs became larger, it was also important to strengthen the contact between the hips and the backbone. This was accomplished by increasing the number of vertebrae that had direct attachments to the upper hip bone (ilium). The tail was strengthened to provide a counterbalance for the front of the body.

Opposite page ~ Eoraptor searches the foliage of a Late Triassic forest for insects and other tasty morsels of food. With its long, upright legs and well-balanced body, it was a more sophisticated hunter than any of the thecodonts.

The First Dinosaurs

In 1991, a very important skeleton was collected in northwestern Argentina in 228 million year old rocks. The skull of this small dinosaur has been described subsequently as *Eoraptor* by its discoverer, Dr. Paul Sereno of the University of Chicago. This carnivorous animal, barely more than a metre long, is the most primitive dinosaur yet recovered. It had long legs to help it move quickly, and the hands were equipped with sharp claws to help it capture and kill prey. Like most primitive and carnivorous dinosaurs, the long bones of the limbs were hollow. The skull has large eyes, but strong, recurved teeth. The jaw was relatively straight, and is primitive for a meat-eating dinosaur because it lacks a specialized joint found in theropods. This extra hinge, the intramandibular joint, is found between the front and back halves of the jaw, and was used to increase the gape of the jaw. Because birds are specialized theropods, it is not surprising that they still have this joint. Although *Eoraptor* is anatomically close to the common ancestor of saurischian and ornithischian dinosaurs, it has already become more theropod-like in several characters. For example, the thumb is considered as the first digit of the hand, and the outer finger is the fifth one. Over time, theropod dinosaurs reduced the size and number of their fingers from the outside until only the first two fingers were left in tyrannosaurids and only one finger is left in *Mononykus*. In contrast, ornithischians reduced the first and the fifth fingers. Like theropods, *Eoraptor* reduced its outer two fingers in size.

Until recently, another dinosaur from Argentina called *Herrerasaurus* was thought to have been the best candidate as a common ancestor for all dinosaurs. However, the discovery of a new and better specimen has shown that it is a primitive theropod. It is more advanced than its contemporary *Eoraptor* as it has a joint in the middle of its lower jaw. The skull was relatively big, and the jaws were lined with the sharp teeth of

There are a number of characters in the skull of *Eoraptor* that show it was a meat-eating animal. Nevertheless, it lacks the joint in the middle of the jaw that characterizes all later theropods.

Paul Sereno (University of Chicago) found the skeleton of *Eoraptor*, the most primitive dinosaur presently known, in Upper Triassic rocks in Argentina.

The rich Triassic ecosystems of Brazil have changed little in appearance, but Staurikosaurus would not be able to survive if brought back to life. But in its time, it was a well-adapted soldier in the struggle for existence.

There is little comparison between the forested environments where Herrerasaurus hunted, and the modern desert environment east of the Andes where its fossil remains are found.

The skull of *Herrerasaurus* shows most of the characteristics of a carnivorous dinosaur, including a joint halfway along the lower jaw that allowed some movement between the front and back.

a meat-eater. Only three vertebrae had been incorporated into the hips. The hip socket, like those of all dinosaurs, has a hole on the inside wall, but the opening is relatively small compared to most other dinosaurs. Like more advanced theropods, the pubic bone is elongate and is conspicuously widened at the distal end into what is often called a pubic boot. The upper leg bone, the femur, was longer than the shin (tibia), suggesting that it was a much slower animal than later theropods. Front and hind feet had five toes each, terminating in blunt claws. The bones are surprisingly similar to those of more advanced theropods.

For many years after its discovery, it was believed that *Herrerasaurus* was primitive enough to be ancestral to both lizard-hipped and bird-hipped dinosaurs. Derived characters in the skull and skeleton are known now that show it was unquestionably a theropod.

Staurikosaurus is a 2 m long carnivorous dinosaur of about the same age as *Eoraptor* and *Herrerasaurus*. The head of this Brazilian animal was as long as its upper leg bone, and there were 13 or 14 sharp teeth in each lower jaw. The front limbs were somewhat short and terminated in five digits. There are only two vertebrae attached to the hip bones, which is a very primitive characteristic (most theropods have five sacral vertebrae). The hind leg was long and erect. The lower leg bones were longer than the upper, which is common in animals that run fast. It was a slender, active predatory animal, weighing about 30 kg. Although relatively small, it was probably capable of bringing down and killing larger animals.

A few years ago, a great deal of publicity was generated by a discovery in Petrified Forest National Park of Arizona. A partial skeleton of a staurikosaur, named Gertie after the dinosaur in the first animated cartoon, showed that these animals lived in North America as well.

Eoraptor, Herrerasaurus and *Staurikosaurus* show how carnivorous dinosaurs were evolving 225 million years ago. Herbivorous dinosaurs start to appear in the fossil record at the same time. *Pisanosaurus* is based on a fragmentary skull and skeleton from Argentina. The teeth are closely packed to form a continuous surface for chopping up plants. The crown of each tooth is expanded at the base, giving it a leaf-like appearance. Similar teeth are found in the contemporary *Technosaurus* from Texas. These basal ornithischians are better understood when they are compared with a slightly later form, *Lesothosaurus* from the Lower Jurassic of South Africa. In addition to having the typical leaf-shaped teeth of a herbivore, this dinosaur has one of the most obvious characteristics of an ornithischian dinosaur. The predentary is an extra (new) bone at the front of the lower jaws. It is usually beak-like, lacks teeth, and separates the left and right jaws. Five vertebrae form the sacrum for attachment to the hips, which are clearly the bird-hipped form of an ornithischian. The terminal joints of the toes are more claw-like than hoof-like.

As indicated by discoveries in northwestern Argentina, the Late Triassic was a highly important time for the origin of dinosaurs. Dinosaur remains are not common there, but every find is extraordinarily valuable. As early as 225 million years ago, dinosaurs had already split into the Saurischia and the Ornithischia. It is clear dinosaurs developed from small, running bipedal reptiles. They evolved rapidly, perhaps explosively. Initially, dinosaurs showed their greatest improvements in the hind limbs and their

The discovery of a partial skeleton of a dinosaur in the Triassic rocks of Petrified Forest in Arizona caused a stir in 1985. Nicknamed Gertie, this specimen showed that staurikosaurs were widespread 225 million years ago. White dots in the silhouette above are actual bones of Gertie found.

Previous page ~ Like ghosts in the forest, Syntarsus creeps quietly through the underbrush. In Africa and North America, these animals would occasionally gather into large packs, perhaps to ensure mating and reproductive success.

abilities to move quickly and efficiently. Later dinosaurs would show physiological and behavioural improvements that helped them to maintain their dominance of the land until the end of the Cretaceous.

Before the end of the Triassic, some 210 million years ago, something extraordinary happened on our planet. The climate cooled and numerous groups of animals died out. Only small forms survived. The extinction was the result of climatic changes, orogenetic processes and the origin of new seas. After the period of destruction at the end of the Triassic, the climate improved, new sources of food evolved, and new habitats opened up. The coincidental development of these favourable circumstances is believed to have led to the explosive radiation of the dinosaur population on the Earth.

Diversification of Dinosaurs

Skeletal remains from Triassic rocks suggest that dinosaurs rapidly evolved into three major lineages. Although theropods are perhaps more primitive animals, the earliest ones are not significantly older than the earliest ornithischians. By the end of the Triassic, the diversity and number of dinosaurs had increased conspicuously, and they were clearly the dominant land animals. Saurischian (lizard-hipped) dinosaurs included the carnivorous theropoda, which walked erect on two legs and developed into enormous forms like *Tyrannosaurus rex* and birds, and the herbivorous sauropodomorphs, which mostly walked on all four legs and included such giant forms as *Apatosaurus*, *Diplodocus*, and *Brachiosaurus*. Ornithischian (bird-hipped) dinosaurs generally have a toothless beak at the front of the jaws, grinding teeth, facial pouches and a special bone at the tip of their lower jaw. The backbone is strengthened with ossified tendons.

The earliest ornithischians presently known are recovered from the same rocks that produce the earlierst saurischians. A new bone at the front of the lower jaw is one of the easiest ways to show that animals like *Lesothosaurus* are ornithischians.

EARLY DINOSAURS

Eoraptor. The most primitve dinosaur presently known. Late Triassic of Argentina.

Herrerasaurus. Late Triassic of Argentina.

Ischisaurus. Late Triassic relative of *Herrerasaurus* from Argentina.

Lesothosaurus. An early form of ornithischian living during the Early Jurassic in Lesotho.

Pisanosaurus. A Late Triassic ornithischian from Argentina.

Staurikosaurus. From the Late Triassic of Brazil.

Technosaurus. This primitive ornithischian lived during the Late Triassic in what is now the United States.

Liliensternus was an Upper Triassic theropod from Germany. Originally described by F. von Huene in 1943 as Halticosaurus, this animal was closely related to Coelophysis and Syntarsus. The two partial skeletons that have been found suggest it was a small to medium-sized dinosaur.

Theropoda

Theropoda include bipedal meat-eaters which, like modern carnivores, were much rarer than any of the herbivorous forms. At one time all of the small carnivores were referred to as coelurosaurs, and all of the large forms were called carnosaurs. However, this was a gross simplification that did not reflect the relationships. Small forms like *Syntarsus* and *Coelophysis* are more closly related to *Dilophosaurus* and *Ceratosaurus* than they are to later small carnivores like *Dromaeosaurus*. It also appears that *Tyrannosaurus* is genetically more similar to small forms like *Troodon* and *Ornithomimus* than it is to *Allosaurus*. Theropods survived from Late Triassic to Late Cretaceous times.

Small theropods were generally lightly built, and must have been relatively agile animals. Some were no bigger than chickens; others exceeded an ostrich in size. They fed on insects, lizards, mammals, eggs, young dinosaurs and anything else they could capture. In their time, they were also a sort of sanitary police, eating the carcasses of other animals that died from natural causes. Small theropods probably gave rise to birds.

Coelophysis is one of the best known early species, and is represented by more than a hundred specimens from the Upper Triassic Ghost Ranch site of New Mexico, which was discovered in 1947. It attained a length of 3 m and weighed about 30 kg. At least twelve skeletons were complete, and represent young individuals as well as adults. The finding of so many skeletons on one site suggests these dinosaurs might have lived in a pack that died together. *Coelophysis* seems to have inhabited highland forests. Their prey might have included labyrinthodont amphibians, several types of relatively primitive reptiles, prosauropod dinosaurs and mammal-like reptiles. It is interesting that two adult skeletons also contained the bones of small individuals of the same species, suggesting cannibalistic behaviour.

These Upper Triassic theropods must have been wild, predatory hunters, as their skeletons indicate that they were built for running faster than the contemporary herbivores. Their bones were hollow, and their rear legs were strong and long. The neck was slender, and the tail was about one half of the total body length. The long, narrow head was armed with numerous sharp teeth, each of which had serrated edges. Each front limb had four fingers, although only three were strong enough for capturing prey. The hind leg, similar to the bird's leg, had three main toes with sharp claws

Liliensternus (=*Halticosaurus*) is larger than the closely related *Coelophysis*, attaining a length of 5.5 m. Skeletal remains were found in the Upper Triassic of southern Germany, while footprints attributed to the same animals have been found in the Upper Triassic beds of Slovakia. They were robust animals, with big heads, large orbits and pointed snouts. The tail was long, with elongate distal vertebrae. The pubic bone was as long as the femur, and was thickened at the distal end. The ischium was shorter and more slender, but was also thickened at the distal end. Like other theropods, the first and fifth toes of the hind foot were reduced.

Other families of small theropods (including dromaeosaurids, elmisaurids, oviraptorids and troodontids) did not appear until the Jurassic and Cretaceous, when

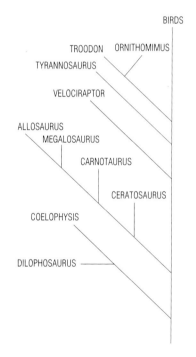

At one time it was assumed that theropods could be divided into only two lineages. The large theropods like *Allosaurus* and *Tyrannosaurus* were called carnosaurs, while all small theropods were identified as Coelurosauria. We now know that this was a simplistic approach for such a successful group, which survived for 160 million years, and newer classifications have many more branches.

they became widespread. Large carnivores, characterized by *Allosaurus*, did not appear until the Jurassic. Reports of large Triassic theropods have invariably turned out to be either herbivorous prosauropods or rauisuchian thecodonts.

Sauropodomorpha

Sauropodomorphs include both prosauropods and sauropods. The former are generally, but not universally, considered to be ancestral to the latter. Certainly they did occupy similar ecological niches, and there is no doubt that sauropods replaced prosauropods.

Prosauropods are the most primitive of the generally quadrupedal, herbivorous dinosaurs. They were successful animals, that, during Late Triassic and Early Jurassic times, colonized all regions of their world, and have been found in Argentina, Canada, China, France, Germany, Great Britain, Greenland, Lesotho, Morocco, South Africa, Switzerland, the United States and Zimbabwe. Some were extremely large animals for their time, but would have been considered as small animals compared to virtually all sauropods.

Plateosaurids are the best known family of prosauropods. They were much bigger than other Late Triassic dinosaurs. The skull was larger and stronger than that of other prosauropods, although it was still relatively small compared to the rest of the body. They walked on all four limbs as a rule, but could have risen up onto their stout hind legs when reaching for a particularly tasty morsel in the bushes or trees. When erect on their hind legs, prosauropods like *Plateosaurus* may have reached 3 m off the ground. They may also have run on their hind limbs, balanced by their long tails, when trying to escape predators. Unfortunately, they probably could not maintain their bipedal pose for long because of their relatively great size as adults. The best known genus was *Plateosaurus*, whose numerous skeletons have been found in Europe. They were up to 7.5 m long, much of which was neck and tail. The teeth were leaf-shaped with saw-tooth serrations along the front and back margins. Three vertebrae (sacrals) connected the backbone to the hips. The pubis, the front bone of the lower part of the hips, was long and narrow, and did not expand at the end into a conspicuous boot as it does in many theropods. The front limbs, like those of most dinosaurs, were shorter than the hind ones, but were still very strong and were equipped with five fingers. The first finger was stouter than the others and terminated in a large claw that may have been used as a defensive weapon. The fourth and fifth, or outer, fingers were reduced in size, and like most prosauropods did not bear claws. The tendency for the inner fingers to be more powerfully developed than the outer ones is also typical of theropods and sauropods.

The best discoveries of *Plateosaurus* were made in the first half of the 20th century, and were largely the result of the efforts of Professor Friedrich von Huene from the University of Tübingen in Germany. These finds included individual skeletons, skeletons in bonebeds, isolated bones and teeth, and footprints. At some sites, the trackways of numerous *Plateosaurus* individuals are moving in a single direction. Massive accumulations of bones in bonebeds show that plateosaurs sometimes died together, which in turn suggests that they were living together in herds. Although more than

Coelophysis is the best known dinosaur from the Triassic, and hundreds of skeletons have been collected from Ghost Ranch in New Mexico. The original fossil was collected from a different site, however, and is very incomplete. Because it is difficult to know if specimens from the two sites represent the same species, some palaeontologists believe the Ghost Ranch material should be given a different name (*Rioarribasaurus*).

twice the length of contemporary predators, they lacked weapons to ward off the attacks of hungry carnivores. Herding provided them with greater security. Von Huene was the first to suggest that herding may indicate migratory behaviour for some species of dinosaurs.

Like most animals, including man, prosauropods had a tendency to increase their size as they evolved over time. This had several advantages, including the determent of carnivorous theropods. This tendency towards gigantism also may have been a response to hard climatic conditions at the end of the Triassic. According to Bergmann's rule, there is a selective advantage in reducing the relative surface area of a body living in cold climatic conditions. Because larger animals have a relatively smaller ratio of surface area to muscular bulk than smaller animals, they can retain stable body temperatures better. This means that it would take longer to overheat when it is hot, or to cool down when the ambient temperature of the air is cold. Large dinosaurs therefore had relatively stable body temperatures, and would not have required insulation like hair or feathers to maintain constant body temperatures.

Anchisaurids were another family of prosauropods that were widely distributed in Late Triassic and Early Jurassic times. They were smaller, reaching lengths of some 2.5 m. Several characters distinguish this family from other prosauropods, including the fact that the claw on the first (inside) toe of the foot has been reduced so that it is smaller than the claw of the second toe.

Other prosauropod families include thecodontosaurids (Great Britain, Morocco), massospondylids (southern Africa), and yunnanosaurids (China).

Dinosaurs at the End of the Triassic

Dinosaurs began their evolution more than 225 milion years ago, and except for the birds, died out almost 65 million years before man appeared. As the dominant land animals for 160 million years, they were unquestionably the most successful animals that ever evolved. Dinosaurs evolved at a time when all the continents formed one supercontinent, Pangaea. This allowed them to proliferate quickly over all land masses. By the end of the Triassic, they were already diversifying and increasing in size, hints of the success that would follow throughout the Jurassic and Cretaceous.

The first dinosaurs probably looked like carnivorous theropods, which are the most conservative dinosaurs and most closely resemble the thecodont ancestors of all dinosaurs. The advances in limb structure probably gave dinosaurs like *Staurikosaurus* and *Eoraptor* the advantage when they were competing with more primitive, non-theropod thecodonts. This increased their success in finding and taking food, and made them the most competitive animals of that time. By the end of the Triassic, dinosaurs had become the dominant land animals. Some speculate that they acquired this advantage through direct competition, whereas others maintain that they were the survivors of an unspecified natural catastrophe that eliminated their competitors.

MESOZOIC	**CRETACEOUS**		
	JURASSIC		
			213 mya
	TRIASSIC	LATE	231 mya
		MIDDLE	243 mya
		EARLY	248 mya

The Mesozoic Era is often referred to as the Age of Dinosaurs. The earliest of the three periods in the Mesozoic was the Triassic, which lasted from 248 to 213 million years ago. Dinosaurs appeared about 230 million years ago during the last half of the period.

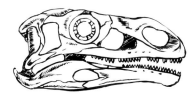

Plateosaurus is one of the best known prosauropods, and many specimens have been collected in Europe, especially Germany. The teeth are relatively simple, but were suited to chopping up plants coarsely.

Opposite page ~ First of the large herbivores, prosauropods like the European Plateosaurus were the most common dinosaurs by the end of the Triassic.

THE MIDDLE OF THE MESOZOIC ~ THE JURASSIC PERIOD

During the 72 million year span of the Jurassic Period, great changes occurred in the positions of the continents. At the beginning of the period, Pangaea still existed as a single land mass. However, Tethys was penetrating ever more deeply into the slowly sinking area between the African plateau and Laurasia. As early as the beginning of the Jurassic, the seas extended over vast regions of Europe and Asia. The first connection between Tethys and the Pacific coast of Pangaea, and the beginning of the opening of the Atlantic took place during early Jurassic transgressions of the seas onto land. In this way, Pangaea was separated into the northern continent Laurasia, and the southern continent Gondwanaland. The latter was further subdivided into smaller continents later in the Jurassic.

Because of the enormous expanses of water that covered vast regions of Europe and Asia, the mild and rather arid climates of the Triassic became humid and warm during the Jurassic. Even the relatively wide equatorial zone from Greenland to South Africa was characterized by consistent temperatures. The mean sea water temperatures were between 20° and 30°C. Towards the polar regions, the oceanic waters were cooler, but were still above 10°C, and there were no polar ice caps.

Flora

Jurassic flora was slowly evolving and changing. Because the continents were interconnected, known floras are widespread. Characteristic tree-ferns were found in the tropics, whereas lower herbaceous forms dominated in the cooler climatic zones of places like Siberia.

Ferns of the family Dipteridaceae were common and widespread in the Early Jurassic, and representative forms include *Thaumathopteris* and *Clathropteris*. They are thought to be characteristic of moist, warm conditions. Other ferns (Caytoniales, Matoniaceae) and horsetails, including *Equisetites munsteri*, were successful. The Bennettitales, a group of gymnosperms related to modern cycads, proliferated during the Jurassic. Conifers like *Podozamites* and *Ginkgo* formed the primeval forests of the Asian continent. The predecessors of pines, cedars, sequoias and cypresses can be found in the Jurassic, whereas *Araucaria* (Araucariaceae) and yews (Taxodiaceae) were already established. In Patagonia, whole forests of fossilized araucarians and taxodiaceous (*Paraucaria*) trees have been preserved. Ferns abounded around Tethys and towards the east.

In the seas, algae were evolving and spreading. Some of these (*Solenopora*, Dasycladaceae) continued to be very important plants in the formation of limestones.

The teeth of *Plateosaurus* are leaf-shaped with serrations along the front and back margins. This form of tooth is widespread in primitive plant-eating dinosaurs, both saurischian and ornithischian.

One of the smallest known dinosaurs is a prosauropod baby from the Late Triassic of Argentina. A baby *Mussaurus* skeleton is small enough to fit in the palm of the hand.

Fauna

The dinosaurs were not the only characteristic animals of the Jurassic. Protozoans known as foraminifera were widespread, and corals were diversifying. Their propagation in the warm seas of that time is evident in the huge, fossilized coral reefs. Numerous other animals, such as molluscs, siliceous sponges and bryozoans, contributed to the formation of the reefs. Brachiopods, on the other hand, were less common, replaced by Lamellibranchia. The most important invertebrates were the ammonites, which had almost died out at the end of the Triassic. One group, the Phylloceratidae, survived the extinctions, and ammonites underwent an explosive radiation in the Jurassic.

Crinoids were still common in some regions in the shallow seas. They were mostly anchored to the sea beds, but there were also some freely floating forms. Asteroidea, Ophiuroidea, crabs and other crustaceans were successful.

Fresh waters on land, and salt waters of the sea were inhabited by a variety of fish. The bodies of some were protected by thick, bony scales. Sharks and rays continued to be successful, and were not much different from modern forms. Domination of the waters was held by marine reptiles, including ichthyosaurs and plesiosaurs. *Elasmosaurus* was one of the largest plesiosaurs from North America, and had a length of 13 m.

Jurassic marshes, swamps and lakes were the habitats of the first true frogs. The earliest records of frogs are from northern Spain (*Palaeobatrachus, Discoglossus*) and Argentina (*Notobatrachus, Vieraella*).

Today, most crocodilians are restricted to fresh water environments. But in the Jurassic, crocodiles like *Metriorhynchus* and *Geosaurus* lived in the seas. The marine crocodiles were perfectly adapted for swimming, with fins on their tails and limbs

PROSAUROPODS

Coloradisaurus. Late Triassic. Argentina.

Mussaurus. Late Triassic. Argentina.

Sellosaurus. Late Triassic. Germany.

Thecodontosaurus. Late Triassic. Great Britain.

Ammosaurus. Early Jurassic. Canada, United States.

Anchisaurus. Early Jurassic. United States.

Lufengosaurus. Early Jurassic. China.

Massospondylus. Early Jurassic. South Africa, United States, Zimbabwe.

Massospondylus, one of the better known prosauropods, had relatively simple dentition for chopping up vegetation.

Following page ~ Herds of Apatosaurus kept even the tallest trees well-trimmed. They would have been unconcerned about the presence of Camptosaurus browsing on ground vegetation, but undoubtedly kept watch for prowling theropods.

adapted into paddles. All crocodilians were not large, and some appear to have become primarily land dwellers. In the shallow seas of some regions, small forms like *Alligatorium* (40 cm in total length) and *Alligatorellus* (22 cm long) fed on invertebrates and small fish.

Dinosaurs in the Jurassic

Sauropoda

The sauropods first appeared early in the Jurassic, and are assumed to have been descended from prosauropod ancestors. There are some problems with this assumption, however, and it is possible that they evolved independently from a common ancestor. Whereas prosauropods disappeared early in the Jurassic, sauropods continued to diversify throughout the Jurassic and the Cretaceous.

Massospondylus, one of the better known prosauropods, had a relatively slim but tall skull. The recovery of fossils of this animal in both Africa and North America shows that there were connections between these two continents 210 million years ago.

MESOZOIC	CRETACEOUS		
			144 mya
	JURASSIC	LATE	163 mya
		MIDDLE	188 mya
		EARLY	213 mya
	TRIASSIC		

The Mesozoic Era lasted from 248 to 65 million years ago. It is divided into three periods (Triassic, Jurassic and Cretaceous), each of which is further subdivided. The middle period, the Jurassic, is characterized by the largest known dinosaurs.

Hunting late into the evening, a hungry Dilophosaurus was the undisputed ruler of early Jurassic times in China and the United States. A double crest on top of the skull served as its crown.

Sauropods were the largest animals to have lived on land, attaining possible lengths of more than 50 meters (*Seismosaurus*), and weights estimated to have been as high as 80 tonnes. The long sauropod neck ended in a relatively small head. Although the head of a sauropod looks miniscule, it did not need to be any larger because it served as little more than an extension of the throat, and a place to position the eyes, nose, ears and the relatively small brain.

There was a lot of variability in the sizes and positions of sauropod nostrils. In most forms they are situated high on the side of the face, but in *Diplodocus* they merged and were found at the top of the head between the eyes. The high positions of the nostrils are similar to those of animals like elephants and tapirs, which have elongated the fleshy parts of their noses and upper lips. This has led some scientists to the conclusion that there may have been a proboscis to help the sauropod collect leaves from the tops of trees. Earlier on, scientists had suggested that the high positions of the nostrils were an indication of the aquatic habits of sauropods. It is unlikely that the head and neck could have served as a snorkel, however, because the water pressure on the sides of the body would have prevented an animal from breathing if it was too far underwater. Robert Bakker has suggested that the large nostrils of sauropods may have enclosed extended nasal canals for moistening and filtering inhaled air, and for increasing the nasal epithelia to improve the sense of smell. Nasal salt glands may also have been present, as in modern desert lizards like *Varanus griseus*. The large sizes of the nostrils of the prosauropod *Massospondylus* can be correlated with the arid environments of the Late Triassic, supporting the concept of nasal salt glands in sauropodomorphs.

During the Jurassic, the continents were in the process of breaking apart into smaller units. The continental mass in the north is known as Laurasia, whereas that of the southern hemisphere is called Gondwanaland.

Because most of the food processing was done in the gut, teeth are simple and lacked crushing or grinding surfaces. They were either peg-like, or spoon-shaped, and there were never more than a dozen teeth on each side of the mouth. The teeth may have been used to strip the leaves off of branches high in the trees, or to collect softer, more herbaceous plants near the ground. It is almost unbelievable that the relatively weak dentition of sauropods was capable of providing the enormous quantities of food these colossi would have required for their upkeep. However, the teeth and jaws only gathered the food, which was subsequently ground up in the muscular gut by a huge mass of stones swallowed for the purpose. The ingested stones (gastroliths), which became highly polished as they rubbed against each other in the digestive acids, have been found within the rib cages of *Seismosaurus* and other sauropods. Because modern birds lack teeth, many have developed a similar system for processing plant food. As in all modern plant-eaters, digestion of plant material would have been aided by micro-organisms living in the digestive tract.

Ammonites are related to modern squid, octopus and *Nautilus*, and probably had the same characteristic tentacles. They were more diverse and numerous in the seas than dinosaurs were on land.

Relative to the enormous body, the brain of a sauropod was unbelievably small. However, bigger animals have always relatively smaller brains, and even within our own species the brain of a baby is a much higher percentage of body weight than it is in an adult. The larger body of a sauropod has no more joints or muscles than much smaller animals, so the number of movements being controlled is the same. And as we know with computers, bigger is not necessarily better. Study of sauropod biology suggests that they had quite complex behaviour, and their brains were obviously adequate, and capable for doing more than we generally give them credit for.

An expansion of the spinal cord in the hips has often been referred to as a second brain that was required to control the back end of the body. Although the sacral expansion was much larger than the brain (in the head), it would not have had the ability to think and control. In fact, similar expansions of the spinal canal are found in the hips of migratory birds, where they are used to store a highly efficient source of food energy.

A sauropod neck can be extremely long, especially in forms like *Mamenchisaurus*, whose neck makes up 40% of the total body length. There are 12 to 19 neck vertebrae in sauropods, each of which can be up to 1.5 m long. Weight reduction is one reason that the head of a sauropod is small, because a larger skull on the end of such a long neck would be more difficult to support. The neck vertebrae are extremely light compared to those of the trunk and tail. This is because there are air sacs that extend from the lungs along the side of the neck and into each vertebra. The neck vertebrae, then, are like air filled balloons of very thin bone, and are marvellously engineered structures for lightness and strength.

The thoracic region of a sauropod is relatively short, and is made up of only a dozen or so vertebrae. Four to six vertebrae are fused together between the hips, whereas the tail can have as many as 80 vertebrae.

There is a single spine on top of each vertebra in most animals with backbones, including primitive sauropods like *Cetiosaurus*. Vertebral spines are interconnected by ligaments, which help control the amount of bending along the backbone. In some of the more advanced sauropods, the neural arches at the base of the neck are split into two, separated on the midline by a deep cleft. It is believed that powerful ligaments, attached to muscles, ran along the bottom of the trough between the spines. The combination, which is reminiscent of a pulley and cable system, would have been used to raise the neck. In *Barosaurus*, the spines are split as far back as the hips, suggesting that this animal could pull itself up onto its back legs.

Left ~ Vulcanodon has often been called the link between prosauropods and sauropods. However, most workers now believe this Early Jurassic African animal is a true sauropod.

Opposite page ~ As storm clouds gather over ancient India, Barapasaurus looks fearfully for a safe haven where it will not be the highest point for lightning to strike. This is only one of the unique problems such huge animals must have had.

The elongate tails may have been used as weapons. In forms like *Diplodocus*, the tails are long and whiplike, whereas some of the Chinese species had small bony clubs at the ends of their tails. Their strong limbs were columnar, and were held vertically beneath the body. The front legs were substantially shorter than the hind in all sauropods except the brachiosaurs. Each hand had five fingers, and each foot five toes. The digits were relatively short, but there was a tendency for the inside ones to bear the largest claws.

At one time it was believed that sauropods were too massive to carry their weight on land, so they lived mostly in water where their bodies would have been lifted by the weight of the displaced water. However, little evidence has been found to support this theory. Analysis of the skeleton shows that the limbs and girdles are similar to those of land living animals like elephants, and there is no evidence of special adaptations that would have helped sauropods swim. The feet are too narrow to have been much use in walking across the mud. Finally, sauropods inhabited a wide range of environments, but many of these were arid or semi-arid, and there would not have been any large bodies of water for them to swim in.

Wherever sauropods lived, the food had to be plentiful, and these animals were probably eating almost constantly. Estimates of their daily food intake are widely variable, ranging from a few hundred kilograms to the unlikely estimate of half a tonne.

Trackway sites show that at least some sauropods congregated into herds, like elephants and other large mammals. It has even been suggested that the herds were structured, so that the juveniles were always surrounded by adults for protection.

Although sauropods lived throughout the Jurassic and Cretaceous, they reached their peak of diversity and size during Late Jurassic times. They are best known in the western United States, where the giants included the longest (*Seismosaurus*) and

The nostrils of a sauropod were positioned high on the skull, in a similar position to those of an elephant and a tapir. Because both of these mammals have long flexible trunks, it is conceivable that a sauropod like *Camarasaurus* may have had a proboscis like an elephant.

The elongate tails of sauropods may have been used as weapons. In forms like *Diplodocus*, the tails are long and whiplike, whereas the Chinese *Omeisaurus* had a small bony club at the end of the tail.

Previous page ~ Sauropods like Brachiosaurus did not need water to buoy up their weight, and when they swam their bodies would have floated near the surface. This is one of many reasons that palaeontologists believe the long neck of a sauropod was not used to raise the head above the surface of the water as it walked on the bottom. A pair of young plesiosaurs have come upstream from the sea to fish, and to rid themselves of bothersome parasites that do not like the fresh water.

heaviest (*Ultrasauros*) land animals ever known. However, they appear to have also reached their peak of development at the same time in other parts of the world, especially China.

One of the earliest sauropods was *Vulcanodon*, from the Lower Jurassic deposits of Zimbabwe. Although information is not complete, it appears to have been about 6 m long. Unlike its ancestors, *Vulcanodon* was a quadrupedal animal. A contemporary from India, *Barapasaurus*, was larger, attaining a length of 18 m. Unlike prosauropods, but like all later sauropods, the neck vertebrae of *Barapasaurus* were hollowed out for extensions from the lungs.

Cetiosauridae

Cetiosaurids are the most primitive of the well-known sauropod families. Specimens have been described from Australia, Great Britain, Morocco and the United States, but they are best known from more than 20 skeletons recovered in southern China (Zigong, Sichuan) in recent years. *Shunosaurus* was 19 m long, had jaws with spoon-shaped teeth, and large paired nostrils positioned high on the head. An interesting characteristic is the fusion of vertebrae and bony plates at the end of the tail to form a tail club that was probably used to defend itself against predators. Like other sauropods, cetiosaurids attained great size. Footprints in Morocco suggest the presence of an animal with an estimated weight of 60 tonnes.

Cetiosaurids were the dominant sauropods for more than half of the Jurassic. From them arose two lineages, one (Camarasauridae) with the spoon-shaped teeth and relatively stocky bodies of their ancestors, and the other (Diplodocidae) having peg-like teeth, shorter legs, and elongate bodies with long, slender tails. The reason for the divergence was probably related to feeding preferences. The camarasaurids may have preferred to find their food high in the trees, whereas the diplodocids may have carried their heads close to the ground to pasture on low herbaceous plants.

Haplocanthosaurus is a Late Jurassic sauropod that is usually considered as a late surviving cetiosaurid. Found in the United States, it attained a length of 14 m, a height of 3 m, and a weight of approximately 7 tonnes.

Diplodocidae

The best known diplodocid sauropod is the well-known, popular *Apatosaurus*, although it is probably better known by its incorrect, scientifically abandoned name of "*Brontosaurus*". The first skeleton was discovered in 1898 in Wyoming (western United States) near a well-known dinosaur site called Bone Cabin Quarry. This skeleton was assembled in Yale University, but others subsequently appeared in other American museums. Initially, a skull of *Camarasaurus* that was discovered in the same area was put on the skeleton. But this proved to be a mistake, and it is now known that the skull looked more like that of *Diplodocus*. *Apatosaurus* attained a length of 18 m, and was about 5 m high at the hips. The brain in its relatively small skull is probably the smallest, in relation to its gigantic body, of all known vertebrates.

Trackways discovered in Texas have been attributed to *Apatosaurus* in the popular literature, although it is not possible to distinguish the footprints of this animal from those of any of its close relatives. Nevertheless, the trackways suggest that these animals travelled in herds, and that the young were kept to the centre of the herd where they could be protected.

It is generally assumed that sauropods were egg-laying animals like other dinosaurs. However, Bakker has presented evidence to suggest that at least some species may have been live-bearers.

Another well-known sauropod is *Diplodocus*, whose remains are also found in the Upper Jurassic Morrison Formation of the United States. Its body form was similar to that of the closely related *Apatosaurus*, but it was longer and more slender. It could grow up to 32 m long, and was at least 4 m high at the hips. An almost complete, very well preserved skeleton of this giant was excavated in Utah for the Carnegie Museum of Natural History in Pittsburgh. The species, *Diplodocus carnegii*, was established in honour of the philanthropist, Andrew Carnegie, who had financed the excavation. This sponsor subsequently had plaster casts of this specimen prepared for many of the great museums in the world. The National Museum in Prague had to refuse this magnificent gift, however, because it had no room large enough for its installation.

Because most of the food processing was done in the gut, teeth of sauropods like *Shunosaurus* (above) and *Euhelopus* (below) are simple. They were used to "comb" the leaves off branches, but not for chewing.

What appears to be the longest known dinosaur was excavated from the Upper Jurassic beds near San Isidro, New Mexico. *Seismosaurus halli* was described in 1991 by David Gillette. At that time, all of the skeleton had not been excavated or prepared, even though work had begun in 1985. The dimensions of its bones suggest that this

Dicraeosaurus was a diplodocid sauropod from the Late Jurassic of Africa. In the past, palaeontologists thought sauropods were semi-aquatic animals, incapable of holding up their own weight on dry land. The evidence now suggests that some lived in very dry regions where there were no large bodies of water.

animal may have been as much as 54 m in length, although it does not appear to have been any taller than its relatives *Apatosaurus* and *Diplodocus*. The tail appears to have been 26 m long, the estimate being based on 25 of the giant vertebrae. The ribs are as much as 2.2 m long, and 230 gastroliths (stomach stones) were discovered in the rib cage. The discovery of stones in the rib cage of *Seismosaurus* provided the most convincing evidence so far that sauropods swallowed rocks to assist in grinding up food. The gastroliths in this specimen were concentrated in two distinct areas along the digestive tract.

According to Gillette, when *Seismosaurus* was feeding, it probably did not raise its long neck to browse in the tree-tops like other sauropods. Instead, it used its long neck to reach plants growing near the ground. This meant that it could reach the plants within a large radius without having to move too much. Gillette believes that these enormous dinosaurs could not hold their heads erect because pumping blood to a height of over 21 m would put excessive strain on the heart. Other scientists, however, have postulated that there may have been accessory pumps (hearts) in the neck.

Most sauropods were enormous animals, and some may have grown to lengths of more than forty metres.

The *Seismosaurus* skeleton was only a third complete, and it is not known if the whole animal was as long as the estimates suggest it was. Although the preserved portions of *Seismosaurus* are well-preserved, it is not uncommon to find only partial skeletons like this. Often, the skeletons were partially destroyed by carnivores, weathering or river-action before being buried and fossilized.

Barosaurus was another diplodocid sauropod. It attained a length of as much as 25 m, and was found in both North America and Africa. It had a low, flat skull, and the nostrils were positioned well back on the skull. The long neck had vertebrae up to a metre long, but the tail was relatively short.

In 1972, the first specimens of *Supersaurus* were recovered from the Dry Mesa dinosaur quarry of western Colorado. The rocks here are of the Upper Jurassic Morrison Formation, which has produced most of the North American sauropod specimens. The shoulder blade of *Supersaurus* is more than 3 m long, suggesting that the length of the animal was in excess of 30 m.

Africa has provided the remains of *Dicraeosaurus*, a relatively small diplodocid that was first described in 1929. Up to 13 m long, *Dicraeosaurus* was about 3 m high. Its fossils have been found in the Upper Jurassic rocks at Tendaguru in Tanzania, and there have been reports of specimens from the Lower Cretaceous of Egypt. Like other diplodocids, the spines of the vertebrae are split for the cable-like, neck-lifting mechanism.

Previous page ~ Two megalosaurid theropods panic Cetiosaurus, a giant sauropod from the Jurassic of England. Unless the sauropod trips, the theropods will have little satisfaction in bringing down and killing such an enormous animal.

Not long ago (1984), a new species of diplodocid was discovered in South America. *Amargasaurus cazaui* differs from other sauropods because its neural spines are enormously elongated in the neck, body and the front of the tail. The neural spines are split from

Right ~ A Camarasaurus baby playfully stirs up a pair of pterosaurs (Comodactylus) as its mother watches for predators. Sauropod babies have relatively shorter necks and larger heads than the adults.

Other diplodocids have been discovered in North America and Asia, and with the exception of *Nemegtosaurus* from the Upper Cretaceous of Mongolia, all are restricted to the Jurassic.

Brachiosauridae

The heaviest sauropods are the brachiosaurids, whose weight estimates can surpass 80 tonnes. These animals have front limbs that are longer than the hind, and their necks appear to have been held high. The heads may have been held 12 m above the ground, which would have given them a tremendous advantage in spotting food and possible enemies. One of the brachiosaurids, *Ultrasauros*, had a shoulder blade that is 2.1 m long.

Brachiosaurid skulls are relatively high, and the nostrils are positioned on top of the head in front of the eyes, and are separated by a thin arch of bone. As in *Mamenchisaurus*, the neck is extraordinarily long, with vertebrae three times longer than those between the shoulders and hips.

Brachiosaurids are known from the Middle Jurassic to the Lower Cretaceous, and were widespread, their skeletal remains having been discovered in Africa, Europe, Madagascar and North America. The first specimen of *Brachiosaurus altithorax* was discovered in the Upper Jurassic Morrison Formation of the United States in the 19th century. The African species, *Brachiosaurus brancai*, was discovered in 1907. The two species differ in many ways, but the American one was longer, heavier and more robust.

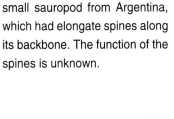

Amargasaurus was a relatively small sauropod from Argentina, which had elongate spines along its backbone. The function of the spines is unknown.

Ultrasauros mcintoshi, sometimes considered to be just a large *Brachiosaurus altithorax*, is a gigantic brachiosaurid discovered in the Dry Mesa Quarry of Colorado. Although only isolated bones have been recovered, they suggest this animal may have been as much as 30 m long. The weight estimates are fantastic, and have been as high as 136 tonnes. Some of the *Brachiosaurus* bones recovered from Africa suggest that some of these animals may have been bigger than *Ultrasauros*.

Brachiosaurids also include the 24 m long *Pelorosaurus* from the Upper Jurassic to Lower Cretaceous rocks of western Europe. The skin of this animal was covered by small hexagonal, flat bumps. The Cretaceous of Morocco and Tunisia was home to *Rebbachisaurus*, a truly gigantic sauropod with 1.5 m long vertebrae.

Animals like Amargasaurus that have crests, frills or other visible displays are usually gregarious, and tend to have complex social behaviour.

The teeth of many sauropods, especially camarasaurids, are often described as spoon-shaped.

The Largest Sauropods

Mamenchisaurus. Late Jurassic, China. The largest dinosaur from Asia, and the longest neck (12 m) known for any animal.

Seismosaurus. Late Jurassic, United States. The longest dinosaur known, perhaps reaching a length of more than 50 m.

Ultrasauros. Late Jurassic, United States. The tallest (15 m) and heaviest (60 tonnes) dinosaur known.

Camarasauridae

Camarasaurid sauropods are believed to have been closely related to brachiosaurids. The best known form is *Camarasaurus*, from the Upper Jurassic Morrison Formation of Colorado, Wyoming and Utah. This animal attained a length of 17.5 m, a height of 3.8 m at the shoulder, and an estimated weight of 30 tonnes. The skull was arched in front of the eyes, and the paired nasal openings were situated high on the skull. The teeth were spoon-shaped. The neural spines of the neck vertebrae, and the first few vertebrae of the trunk, were split. The tail was relatively short. As in all sauropods except for the brachiosaurids, the arms were shorter than the legs. Young *Camarasaurus* specimens have been found, and show that the heads of juveniles were relatively larger, and the neck and legs were relatively shorter than those of the adults.

Asiatosaurus from the Early Cretaceous of Mongolia, *Chiayusaurus* from the Late Cretaceous of China, and *Omeisaurus* from the Late Jurassic of China have also been classified as camarasaurids. The last mentioned genus was over 20 m long, had a more elongate neck than *Camarasaurus*, but had a relatively short skull and spoon-shaped teeth. Three species of *Omeisaurus* have been described, the best preserved of which was *Omeisaurus jungschiensis*. This animal was 14 m long, and had a high skull that was relatively wide at the back. The paired nostrils penetrate a rather prominent snout.

Other possible camarasaurids have been found in Asia. *Opisthocoelicaudia* was recovered by the Polish-Mongolian expeditions from Upper Cretaceous rocks in the Gobi Desert. The 12 m long *Tienshanosaurus* was found by the Sino-Swedish expeditions to northwestern China around 1930. Swedish scientists were also responsible for the discovery of *Euhelopus*, a 14 m sauropod from the Upper Jurassic to Lower Cretaceous beds of eastern China. These and other forms (except *Opisthocoelicaudia* whose head and neck are not known) have broad skulls and spoon-shaped teeth, but these are rather weak criteria for defining a family of dinosaurs.

Theropoda

During the Jurassic, theropods are usually divided into two groups, one characterized by large species, and the other by small forms. However, as more specimens are discovered and palaeontologists learn more about theropod anatomy, it has become increasingly obvious that division of the theropods by size alone is too simplistic. Because large skeletons are less likely to be destroyed before they have a chance to fossilize, it is not surprising that more large species are represented by good skeletons.

Large carnivorous dinosaurs, often referred to as the Carnosauria, did not appear until the Jurassic. Carnosaurs lived mostly in the Jurassic, and did not include the giant tyrannosaurs of the Cretaceous. Most large theropods have similar body plans, developed in response to becoming heavy animals that continued to walk on their hind legs. The skull was large to accommodate an enlarged mouth with relatively large, sharply pointed teeth. Each tooth had a row of saw-like serrations on the front of the tooth, and another row on the back. Although the teeth and jaws probably formed the main weapons of

Opposite page ~ Torvosaurus was a powerful, relatively short-faced Late Jurassic theropod that was probably capable of bringing down small sauropods. As they followed the herd of Ultrasauros, a large male moved between the predators and the potential prey, scaring up a couple of pterosaurs (Comodactylus) in the process.

Meat-eating dinosaurs (thero-pods) had teeth that look like simple cones superficially. However, there are usually ridges along the front and back margins, and these ridges bear sharp, miniature teeth known as denticles or serrations.

large theropods, they were also equipped with powerful, recurved, sharply pointed claws on their hands and feet. The neck was short and strong, and the powerful, sinuous tail functioned as a counterbalance to the head and body in front of the hips. The hands of most carnosaurs have three fingers, but some of the more primitive species had a remnant of a fourth finger. Claws on the feet were large, but tended to end in blunt points that

Above ~ Although it appeared in Late Jurassic times in North America and possibly Africa, Ceratosaurus was a very primitive theropod in most respect. It is not so primitive to realize that it cannot attack Kentrosaurus with impunity, however.

were less likely to be damaged when walking or running. The underside of the belly was supported and in part protected by a cuirass of ventral ribs. These are modified scales inherited from more primitive reptiles, and form a basket underneath the body attached to the ends of the real ribs and to bones of the shoulder and hip girdles.

It is sometimes argued that large theropods were too ponderous to have been hunters, and that they must have been scavengers. However, there are few true scavengers in the world today. Even animals like hyaenas, well adapted to scavenging, need to hunt and kill other animals regularly. It is doubtful that large theropods could find enough food to live if they were restricted to scavenging. Furthermore, rehealed bite marks on the bones of plant-eating dinosaurs demonstrate that the carnivores attacked living animals, which would escape sometimes. Trackway sites also show that carnosaurs followed herbivores, perhaps waiting for stragglers to get separated from the herds.

During the earliest part of the Jurassic, theropods developed elaborate crests on the head, presumably for display. *Dilophosaurus* had a pair of axe-like ridges between the nose and eyes.

Ceratosauridae

Ceratosaurus is probably the most primitive level of Carnosauria, even though this animal did not appear until the end of the Jurassic. It has many primitive characteristics found in smaller theropods from the Early Jurassic, and is considered by some as a close relative of *Coelophysis* and *Syntarsus*. However, like all carnosaurs, *Ceratosaurus* was larger, and had the beginning of a ball-like joint between each of the neck vertebrae.

Following page ~ Even in Middle Jurassic times, disputes would arise between carnivores over food, territories, or potential mates. In most cases, the problems were probably resolved when one of the opponents realized that the other was either bigger or stronger. The fact that fights did occur is demonstrated by the discovery of theropod bones with rehealed bite marks.

Turning away from a half-eaten sauropod carcass, a gorged Allosaurus moves off to find a cool place to sleep.

A horn over the nose is the most characteristic feature of *Ceratosaurus*, which is actually a medium-sized carnosaur that would have weighed less than one tonne. The purpose of the horn is unknown. Some speculate that the males used the horns to butt each other, although the horns are short enough that they are unlikely to have caused any damage. The skull of a *Ceratosaurus* is lightweight, but is more massively built than that of *Allosaurus*. The teeth were unquestionably the major weapons of this animal, although four strong fingers on each hand and three major toes per foot were all armed with sharply pointed, recurved claws.

At present, *Ceratosaurus* is only known from North America, although isolated teeth and bones found in Africa and Asia have also been attributed to this animal.

One of the original bones attributed to *Megalosaurus* was a dentary bone from the lower jaw.

Megalosauridae

Megalosaurids form the largest and most widespread family of Carnosauria, and have been reported from all continents, including Antarctica. Although more than 17 species have been described, most are not well known and it is highly probable that they do not form a natural family. That is, they may represent several distinct families of carnosaurs, but are linked together because they look similar, and because we do not know enough about their histories. Megalosaurids are relatively primitive large theropods, and have relatively long arms. The hand, although known from only a few species, had three functional fingers, but still retained a remnant of the fourth, vestigial finger. Early Jurassic megalosaurids are relatively lightly built animals, whereas later forms like *Torvosaurus* were elephant-sized animals that were probably capable of killing the gigantic sauropods.

The first dinosaur named (in 1822) was *Megalosaurus*. It was a large animal, probably attaining a length of 10 m and a weight of up to 4 tonnes. Many specimens from around the world, including isolated teeth, bones, and footprints have been attributed to this animal, but most of these identifications are unfounded and probably wrong. Several partial skeletons of this animal have been collected in Europe, but have not yet been described, and therefore *Megalosaurus* is still a poorly understood dinosaur. For a long time, palaeontologists thought that it might be as sophisticated as *Allosaurus* from the United States. However, the discovery in China of virtually complete skeletons of related forms show that *Megalosaurus* and its kin were more primitive than *Allosaurus*, although their body forms were quite similar overall.

One of the best known megalosaurs is *Eustreptospondylus*, a medium-sized (5 m) form based on a single incomplete skeleton from the Middle Jurassic of England. The specimen, which is on display at Oxford University, probably represents a juvenile.

Torvosaurus, from the Late Jurassic of the United States, is a relatively large (9 m) and powerfully built megalosaur discovered in the famous Dry Mesa Quarry (near Delta,

Opposite page ~ Monolophosaurus ("one-crested reptile") is a name given in 1993 to a theropod from northwestern China. It is characterized by a low, hatchet-like crest running down the middle of the skull. Like the large depressions on each side of the face, the crest was air-filled to lighten the skull. Here the theropod stretches across some fallen logs to try and retrieve a Peipehsuchus carcass washed up on the shore.

Colorado) along with the giant sauropods *Supersaurus* and *Ultrasauros*. A closely related type, *Edmarka rex*, was described in 1992, and represents an animal that was almost as large as *Tyrannosaurus rex*. It is possible that *Edmarka* is the same as *Torvosaurus*, and the names may be synonymized once more complete specimens are known for both.

Other animals that are generally considered to be megalosaurs are *Poekilopleuron* from the Middle Jurassic of France, *Macrodontophion* from the Jurassic of the Ukraine, and *Szechuanosaurus* from the Jurassic of southern China. Nearly complete skeletons and excellent skulls of megalosaurid-grade theropods have been discovered in the Upper Jurassic rocks of southern and northwestern China. *Sinraptor* and *Yangchuanosaurus* were both more than 8 m long at maturity, but are rather agile looking animals for their size. Together they give us a good understanding of what a megalosaurid is. There is a remnant of the fourth finger in the hand, and the limbs are not as elongate as those of allosaurids.

Allosauridae

The most highly evolved carnosaurs are the allosaurids, a family that includes both *Allosaurus* and *Acrocanthosaurus*. They are considered to be the tigers of the Jurassic and the Early Cretaceous, but were as much as 13 m long with weights in excess of 2 tonnes. Allosaurids are best known from the United States, but specimens have also been reported in Argentina, Australia, China and Tanzania. Unfortunately, few of these specimens are well-enough preserved to determine their relationships with certainty. One of the supposed allosaurids is *Piatnitzkysaurus* from the Middle Jurassic rocks of southern Argentina. Although it superficially resembles *Allosaurus*, closer examination reveals that it belongs to a separate family of theropods (the Abelisauridae) that was evolving independently in the southern hemisphere.

Allosaurids are easily identified by the number of front teeth. Most theropods have four teeth in the premaxillary bone on each side of the mouth. The equivalent teeth in humans are the incisors, and we have two per side. *Allosaurus* is unusual in that it has five premaxillary teeth on each side of the jaw. The giant jaws could open wide enough to inflict serious damage to any animal that was unlucky enough to get caught. The skulls of allosaurids are perhaps a bit lighter than those of megalosaurids, because more of the bones have been invaded by air passages. Compared with more primitive theropods, *Allosaurus* and its kin have one less vertebra in the neck, and one more in the body. Whereas megalosaurids still had the remnants of a fourth finger, allosaurids have only three fingers. The relatively longer legs suggest that these were faster, more sophisticated animals than the megalosaurids. Most of an allosaurid's total length is composed of the tail, which was carried high above the ground to balance the somewhat short, stocky body.

A pack of allosaurid could certainly have killed even a giant sauropod. In one quarry in Utah, the remains of more than 40 allosaurids have been found, and they greatly outnumber the plant eaters. The reason for so many individuals dying at the same site

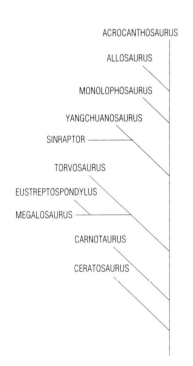

The head of *Yangchuanosaurus* was deep and narrow. Skin would have stretched across the large air pocket between the eye and the nostril, and air pockets invaded many of the bones in the snout.

ACROCANTHOSAURUS

ALLOSAURUS

MONOLOPHOSAURUS

YANGCHUANOSAURUS

SINRAPTOR

TORVOSAURUS

EUSTREPTOSPONDYLUS

MEGALOSAURUS

CARNOTAURUS

CERATOSAURUS

Most large meat-eating dinosaurs are referred to as carnosaurs. These were the dominant carnivores of the Jurassic and Early Cretaceous.

Opposite page ~ Stegosaurs were very successful in southern China during the Jurassic. Tuojiangosaurus is an advanced form that retained two rows of relatively small plates along its back. A spiked plate over the shoulder served as additional protection from carnivores that attempted to attack from the side.

is not understood. Palaeontologists suspect that there may have been a natural predator trap. If a plant-eating dinosaur became trapped in quicksand, tar, or some other substance, its cries would attract carnivores and scavengers. These would in turn get trapped, and attract more carnivores and scavengers. And the cycle would continue, trapping more carnivores than herbivores. The La Brea tar pits in Los Angeles are an example of a well-studied predator trap, although they only date back about 30,000 years.

CARNOSAURS

Acrocanthosaurus. The largest known carnosaur. Lower Cretaceous of Oklahoma and Texas, U.S.A.

Allosaurus. The best known carnosaur, with numerous specimens from the Upper Jurassic Morrison Formation of the western United States.

Eustreptospondylus. A relatively small carnosaur from the Middle Jurassic of England.

Megalosaurus. The first dinosaur described. Middle Jurassic of England and possibly France.

Monolophosaurus. The crest on the skull of this carnosaur is hollow and air-filled. Middle Jurassic, Xinjiang, China.

Piatnitzkysaurus. Most of the skeleton, but little of the skull, of this animal is known. Middle Jurassic of Argentina.

Piveteausaurus. A large theropod from France. Unfortunately, only a partial skull was discovered, so little is known about this animal.

Sinraptor. Known from an almost complete skull and skeleton found in Upper Jurassic rocks in Xinjiang in northwestern China.

Torvosaurus. A powerfully built animal that lived at the same time as *Supersaurus* and *Ultrasauros*. Late Jurassic, Colorado, Utah, U.S.A.

Yangchuanosaurus. Several skeletons with skulls found in Upper Jurassic rocks in Sichuan Province of China.

Following page ~ A placid Hylaeosaurus warily observes a drama unfolding before it as a small theropod (Calamospondylus) attempts to take down an insectivorous pterosaur known as Germanodactylus.

A Hu...
in an...

the...
spe...
cle...
and...

Th...

Th...
arr...
su...
an...
pe...
gr...

th...
ar...
er...
bu...
L...

S...

L...
s...
a...
r...
t...

l...
f...
t...

Ste
low
tee
rat
pla
pe
pie

pairs of vertical plates or spikes of bone along the neck, back and tail. The spikes at the end of the tail are generally considered to have been used for defence. It is unlikely that stegosaurs had the strength to swing it, however. If they wanted to use the tail to fend off an aggressive predator, they would have to swing their bodies away from the attacker. This would bring the tail around and produce a devastating blow if it hit the target.

The best known stegosaur is *Stegosaurus*, from the Upper Jurassic of the western United States. It was up to 8 m in length, and weighed several tonnes. The 3 m height at the hips was mostly made up of the hind legs, which were almost double the length of the arms. The armour plates were up to 76 cm in height, and 79 cm in length. There were four spikes at the end of the tail in *Stegosaurus stenops*. The small brain of

In the Late Jurassic forests of central Asia, Sinraptor has surprised a baby sauropod known as Bellosaurus. Although somewhat more primitive than its relative, Allosaurus, Sinraptor was lightly built and graceful for its giant 7.2 metre length.

Previous page ~ During the Early Jurassic, a primitive armoured dinosaur known as Scelidosaurus appeared in England. Although more lightly built than later Thyreophorans, it may be closely related to the common ancestor of both ankylosaurs and stegosaurs.

Stegosaurus has become almost legendary. Considering the size of this animal, people have long marvelled that it could have a brain as small as a walnut. As it turns out, this is not completely true. When the first cast was done of the inside of a braincase of *Stegosaurus*, there was still a lot of rock inside the skull. A more recent cast has shown that the animal's brain was considerably larger than a walnut, although it is still relatively small for the size of the body. A second legend surrounds the presence of a larger brain in the hips. There is no doubt that there was an expansion of the spinal chord in the hips. However, this was not a second brain. Comparison with other dinosaurs and modern birds suggests it may have been a storage area for a high energy fat reserve. This emergency reserve is used by migratory birds when travelling great distances.

Stegosaur teeth have numerous longitudinal ridges that give the teeth serrated margins. Such teeth are adapted for chewing plants, not meat.

Several partial skeletons of *Dacentrurus* have been collected from Upper Jurassic rocks of England, France and Portugal, but none are complete enough to give a clear understanding of this genus. The tail spikes had sharp edges along both the outside and inside margins. *Kentrosaurus*, from the Late Jurassic of Tanzania, is a relatively small dinosaur with a length of about 2.5 m. Instead of having plates of bone along the back, *Kentrosaurus* had long sharp spikes. In recent years, many new types of stegosaurs have been described from the Jurassic rocks of China. *Huayangosaurus*, the most primitive of these, was only about 4 m long. From the same region of China, but slightly younger in age, *Tuojiangosaurus* was 7 m long, and had as many as fifteen pairs of relatively small plates on its back. *Chungkingosaurus* was recovered from the same region and age, but is distinctive because many of its bony plates were intermediate between plates and spikes. There are four pairs of spikes at the end of the tail.

The function of the giant plates on the back of a stegosaur has been the source of a lot of speculation and discussion over the years. Although generally considered to be a form of defence, the plates do not cover the sides of the animals. Carnivores would have been able to attack the unprotected flanks as long as they could stay away from the tail. Theropods also had extremely powerful jaws that would have had no difficulty in biting through the rather thin plates. Examination of the plates shows that they are covered with canals for blood vessels, and it has been suggested that the plates may have been heat exchangers. If the animal was cold, it would turn so that the sun shone directly on the surfaces of the plates. If the animal was too warm, it would turn perpendicular to the direction of the sun rays. The heat would be picked up or lost by the blood coursing just beneath the surface of the skin that covered the plates.

Stegosaur plates have numerous grooves and canals, showing that they were well supplied with blood vessels. This suggests that they may have been used as heat exchangers, the blood picking up or losing heat on the greatly expanded surface of each plate.

THE CRETACEOUS
~ The Golden Age of Dinosaurs

The Cretaceous is the longest period of the Mesozoic, and lasted a full 71 million years. It is divided into two periods, the Early and Late Cretaceous. The boundary separating it from the Jurassic is vague, and was determined by the retreat of the seas in Europe. The lowermost strata have characteristic lagoonal or terrestrial origins. The end of the Cretaceous, however, is marked very distinctly by the disconformity in the oldest strata of the Tertiary and the earlier beds. This is because of the orogenic activities called Alpine folding. The large mediterranean sea, Tethys, continued to form a warm basin for sedimentation throughout the Cretaceous.

In the Early Cretaceous, the northern and southern continents had already separated. Gondwanaland began to drift away from Laurasia, resulting not only in the enlargement of Tethys, but also the beginning of the North Atlantic Ocean. At the beginning of the Late Cretaceous, the vast Cenomanian transgression began in Europe and on other continents. At the same time, Gondwanaland itself began breaking up. The southern Atlantic Ocean began to separate South America and Africa, and a continent made up of Antarctica, Australia and India pulled away from the other southern continents.

Climatic Conditions

In the Cretaceous, further extension of the surface areas of seas and oceans produced a more effective absorption of solar heat by the Earth. If there were larger sea surface on the Earth today, the water would absorb from 2 to 10 % more heat, which would influence climatic conditions. Dry land on the other hand reflects more solar radiation (between 5 and 30%), and the climatic conditions are cooler. The larger the sea surface in that part of the Earth that is most effectively insolated (the wide equatorial zone from 40° North Latitude to 40° South Latitude), the less heat is reflected back to outer space and the more heat there is to warm the Earth. When most of the continents were in the equatorial zone, the heat balance of the Earth was unfavourably influenced, and cold climates prevailed on land. But in periods when the continental masses had split up and moved away from the equatorial zones, the thermal conditions of the planet were more favourable. The same effect was enhanced when shallow epicontinental seas covered large areas of the continents.

Climatic conditions throughout the Cretaceous were highly favourable, and were more equable than they are today. There were colder periods, but these were of relatively short duration. In the polar regions, there was no persistent ice or snow, although studies of oxygen isotopes in sediments show that temperatures could drop below freezing during winter months. The equatorial/polar gradient (the difference between the average temperatures of the tropics and at the poles) was 22°C, about half of what it is today.

By early Cretaceous times, the continents had separated and were drifting towards their present positions.

Looking more like a crocodile than a theropod because of its long, low skull, Baryonyx may have used the huge, sharp claws on its hands to capture fish in the Early Cretaceous rivers of England. Only one specimen has been found, and it had fish scales inside the rib cage.

Following page ~ Because the climate was warm, mild, and stable, plants that we would consider characteristic of tropical, subtropical and warm temperate regions today lived at much higher latitudes during the Cretaceous. It was an important time in the evolution of flora, as flowering plants (angiosperms) appeared. During the Early Cretaceous, plants like cycads, conifers and Ginkgo helped compose a flora not unlike that of the Jurassic. But between Early and Late Cretaceous times, flowering plants spread across the world and went through amazing diversification. Cycads and Ginkgo lost in competition, and have been greatly reduced in diversity and geographic range.

Dwarfed by dinosaurs like Albertosaurus, mammals remained small throughout the Mesozoic Era. Marsupials like the opossum have changed little since dinosaurs died out, whereas most Mesozoic mammals have been replaced by more progressive forms.

The warmest, most stable period was in the middle of the Cretaceous (Albian times, around 110 million years ago). Since then, the temperatures have been generally dropping to the present day. During the Cretaceous, the levels of the oceans were relatively high in relation to most land masses, partly because of the rise of the mid-Atlantic ridge. Largely because of the polar ice caps, ocean levels are now 250 m below the levels they were in the Cretaceous.

The extraordinarily long duration of favourable climatic conditions led to stable but specialized ecosystems that were ultimately very sensitive to changes in environmental conditions. This is confirmed by the reaction of Cretaceous biota to the relatively small drops in temperature that occurred at the time boundaries between the Albian and Cenomanian (98 million years ago), the Cenomanian and Turonian (91 million years ago) and the Turonian and Coniacian (88 million years ago). These drops in temperature resulted in extinctions, but after each event a new equilibrium was established. The changes at the end of the Cretaceous must have been much greater, because the consequences were catastrophic and irreversible.

Flora

Because the climate was warm, mild, and stable, plants that we would consider characteristic of tropical, subtropical and warm temperate regions lived at much higher latitudes during the Cretaceous. It was also an important time in the evolution of flora, as flowering plants (angiosperms) appeared. During the Early Cretaceous, plants like the cycads and *Ginkgo* contributed to a flora not unlike that of the Jurassic. But between Early and Late Cretaceous times, flowering plants spread across the world and went through amazing diversification. Cycads and *Ginkgo* in particular lost in competition, and have been greatly reduced in both diversity and geographic range.

The evolution of the angiosperms was accelerated by the changing conditions induced by mountain building and transgressions made by epicontinental seas. The more sophisticated reproductive systems of angiosperms allowed them to colonize new areas faster when the seas retreated again.

The origin of angiosperms is still a mystery. They had apparently appeared earlier than the Late Cretaceous. Plants with structures reminiscent of angiosperms are known from sediments in the Upper Triassic of eastern Greenland and the northern Urals. Other angiosperm-like plants are more common in the Jurassic, although it cannot be confirmed that any of these plants had anything to do with the origin of true flowering plants. Most of these plants can be identified as pteridophytes or gymnosperms, and the cycads in particular had obviously made great evolutionary advances since the Permian. For this reason, most palaeobotanists believe that angiosperms had their origins in the class Pteridospermophytina.

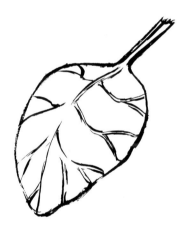

Angiosperms, often referred to as flowering plants, were evolving rapidly and had spread worldwide by the end of Early Cretaceous times. No doubt they had a major influence on the evolution and survival of many groups of dinosaurs.

Late Cretaceous flowering plants include myrtle, magnolia, and sasafras in warmer areas, and beeches, willows, birches and other trees in the higher latitudes.

Fauna

In the Cretaceous seas, protozoans continued to evolve and diversify. The Foraminifera and Flagellata are important as stratigraphic indicators because of all the changes they went through. Sponges and corals abounded, although brachiopods were being reduced in diversity as molluscs proliferated. Oysters, scallops and other types of molluscs can be very common in some rocks. A characteristic Late Cretaceous form is *Inoceramus*. Some inoceramid species from the Canadian arctic and Kansas grew to as much as 2 m across. Snails were widespread. Cephalopods continued to be important in the Cretaceous, although the number of ammonite species was slowly decreasing. Amongst the echinoderms, sessile forms of sea lilies (crinoids) were disappearing, although free floating forms continued to be abundant.

Mammals, contrary to popular belief, had coexisted with dinosaurs since Triassic times. Because they were smaller, and most were probably nocturnal, they escaped the notice of most dinosaurs.

MESOZOIC	CRETACEOUS	LATE	65 mya
			78 mya
		EARLY	144 mya
	JURASSIC		
	TRIASSIC		

The Cretaceous is the last period of the Mesozoic Era. It lasted from 144 to 65 million years ago, and is characterized by the modern appearances of many of the animals and plants.

Sharks, rays and related forms changed slowly into many of the types that are still alive today. Coelacanths were still present, but were clearly in decline. They drop out of the fossil record in the Cretaceous, and were thought to have been extinct until living specimens were found off the coast of Madagascar. The most prolifically evolving fish in the seas were the teleosts, and these remain the most successful fish to this day. The enormous numbers and diversity of Cretaceous fishes were successfully exploited by several types of marine reptiles. Mosasaurs were lizards that went back to the sea, powered by their paddle-like limbs and long, sinuous tails. They resemble their modern relatives, the varanid lizards, in most respects. Mosasaurs were covered by thin scales. Sharp, conical teeth in the jaws and on the roof of the mouth allowed them to capture ammonites, whose shells are often recovered today as fossils with tooth marks.

On land, insects were co-evolving with the flowering plants. Bees, ants, and mosquitoes were just a few of the new innovations. Many modern families of frogs, salamanders, turtles, lizards, snakes, crocodiles, alligators, and birds appeared in the Cretaceous. Mammals were widespread, but remained small and inconspicuous, presumably to avoid competition with the dinosaurs. It appears likely that mammals were active mostly after dark, whereas the majority of dinosaurs were animals of the day. There were exceptions, of course, and it seems highly likely that forms like *Troodon*, with its huge eyes, may have been hunting mammals after sunset. Although many species of Cretaceous mammals were relatively primitive and have no living descendants, some modern lineages of marsupials and placentals, including primates, first appeared at that time. Unfortunately, many of these smaller animals have relatively poor fossil records, even though they were more common animals than dinosaurs. There are many reasons for the poor record. First, small animals tend to be eaten by predators and scavengers, whereas the bones of larger animals are often left behind by meat-eaters. Small specimens are also destroyed by bacterial action and weathering much faster than large skeletons are. Teeth tend to be harder than bones, and these will often be found in concentrations called microvertebrate sites. The size-sorted concentrations can be caused by the action of flowing water, but sometimes are recovered from caves or the coprolites of carnivores.

Right ~ Whereas dinosaurs continued to rule the land throughout the Cretaceous, changes were taking place in the sea and air. Small pterosaurs were gradually replaced by birds, and only the largest flying reptiles escaped direct competition with the feathered dinosaurs. Mosasaurs, closely related to modern varanid lizards, became the dominant marine reptiles.

Dinosaurs

Throughout the Cretaceous, dinosaurs continued to progress, and were far more sophisticated than their Jurassic forebears in feeding mechanisms, limb mechanics, intelligence and behaviour. By Late Cretaceous times, the evolution of plant-eating dinosaurs was probably being driven by the appearance and diversification of flowering plants. Hadrosaurs and ceratopsians were two of the new types of dinosaurs, and they were extremely successful until the end of the Cretaceous.

SAURISCHIA

Titanosaurid sauropods like *Antarctosaurus* were highly successful in the southern hemisphere until the end of the Cretaceous.

Sauropoda

Sauropods were not as diverse during the Cretaceous as they had been throughout the Jurassic, although they continued to exist in most parts of the world. They almost disappeared from North America, but seem to have been making a comeback near the end of the period as titanosaurid sauropods moved in from South America. Titanosaurids, best known from Africa, India, South America, and southern Europe, were most common in the Late Cretaceous. Unfortunately, very few specimens include skull material, and therefore this part of the animal is poorly understood, which makes it difficult for palaeontologists to determine their ancestry. Titanosaurids, including *Saltasaurus* from the Upper Cretaceous of Argentina, had many bony plates in their skin, presumably as a form of armour plating to protect them from carnivores. The rather solid nature of the vertebrae suggests that this group may be much older than its fossil record. The earliest known genus of titanosaurid is *Tornieria* (found in Malawi) from the Upper Jurassic rocks that produced *Brachiosaurus* in Tanzania. Unfortunately, the identification of this animal is based entirely on its tail vertebrae. This is, however, the most important way to identify titanosaurids. These animals have procoelous tail vertebrae; each one has a huge ball-like articulation on the back that fits into a concave depression on the front of the next vertebra. Titanosaurids are generally considered to be the direct descendants of cetiosaurid sauropods, and show relatively little change as flowering plants diversified in the Cretaceous.

Ankylosaurs were not the only armoured dinosarus during Cretaceous times. In South America, titanosaurid sauropods often had bony plates of armour embedded in their skin.

Some titanosaurid species attained considerable lengths. For example, *Aegyptosaurus* from the Upper Cretaceous of Egypt and other parts of northern Africa was about 16 m long, whereas *Aepisaurus* from the Lower Cretaceous of southern France would have been 15 m long. Titanosaurids are rare in North America, so it is ironic that one of the most complete specimens is *Alamosaurus*. This animal, from New Mexico, Texas and Utah, attained a length of 21 m. *Antarctosaurus* is one of the largest dinosaurs, and its femur (upper leg bone) alone is 2.31 m long. In spite of its name, it was found in Argentina, Uruguay and Brazil. Although their name suggests titanosaurids all had titanic dimensions, some types were actually quite small. *Algoasaurus* from Algoa Bay in South Africa is known from relatively few bones, but they suggest that the animal was less than 9 m long. A European Late Cretaceous form, *Hypselosaurus*, was probably only 12 m long. Many of the eggs found in southern France and Spain have been attributed to this titanosaur.

The Cretaceous histories of other groups of sauropods are difficult to determine because of a paucity of good specimens. Camarasaurids seem to have survived in Asia, and *Opisthocoelicaudia* is an Upper Cretaceous representative from Mongolia. The relationship of many of the Asian sauropods to camarasaurids is based on the presence of spatulate, spoon-shaped teeth at the front of the jaws, and it is possible that eventually many of these Asian species may be assigned to a different or new sauropod family. Diplodocids, like *Nemegtosaurus*, appear to have survived until the end of the Cretaceous as well, and have been discovered in China and Mongolia. Like their Jurassic ancestors, they are lightly built for their size, and very long. Their long, low skulls had peg-shaped teeth only at the front of the jaws. *Rebbachisaurus* from the Lower Cretaceous of Morocco is difficult to evaluate because the first specimen discovered consisted of only half a dozen bones. Lower Cretaceous descendants of the gigantic brachiosaurids include *Pelorosaurus* from England, *Pleurocoelus* and *Astrodon* from the United States, and *Chubutisaurus* from South America.

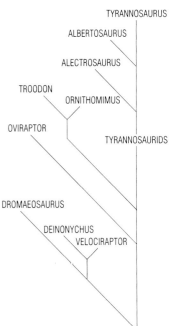

There were many families of theropods during the Cretaceous, just as there are many families of carnivorous mammals today. Tyrannosaurids are more closely related to troodontids, ornithomimids and other small theropods than they are to allosaurids.

Following page ~ Sauropods became extinct in North America early in the Cretaceous. However, towards the end of the period, titanosaurids pushed north from South America and reinvaded the continent. By the end of the Cretaceous, Alamosaurus had spread as far north as Utah.

Saltasaurus, discovered only fifteen years ago in Argentina, proved that sauropods had armour plates in the skin, something that had been suspected since 1896.

Predatory Dinosaurs ~ Theropoda

The fossil record of the Cretaceous is generally better than those of the Triassic and Jurassic, and it is not surprising that we know of many types of predatory dinosaurs. These include the largest meat-eaters to have lived on land and the most sophisticated and highly evolved theropods.

Acrocanthosaurus was the last of the allosaurids, and the largest. The skull can be 1.4 m long, almost as large as that of *Tyrannosaurus*.

Carnosauria

Megalosaurids had disappeared by the end of the Jurassic, although incomplete, unidentifiable specimens from the Cretaceous have sometimes been referred to this family. A good example is *Carcharodontosaurus*, a gigantic but enigmatic theropod from northern Africa that is presently only known from a fragmentary skull and partial skeleton, and isolated teeth and bones. Although the knife-like teeth are similar to those of *Megalosaurus*, some of the bones suggest that it was more advanced, possibly an allosaurid.

Allosaurids did survive into the Early Cretaceous. Although *Allosaurus* itself was extinct by the end of the Jurassic, it was succeeded by *Acrocanthosaurus*. This was an enormous theropod that rivaled *Tyrannosaurus* in size. The skull of one specimen collected in Oklahoma is 1.4 m long, whereas a specimen recently discovered in Texas may even be larger. *Acrocanthosaurus* is unusual in that the neural spines of the backbone are very elongate, although not to the same degree as in the peculiar African form known as *Spinosaurus*.

Tyrannosauridae

The largest and most highly feared of all the theropods was *Tyrannosaurus rex*. This enormous animal was more than 5 metres high and 14 metres long, and would have weighed as much as the largest known bull elephant. The skull could be up to 1.55 m long, which gave it an enormous mouth capable of tearing hundred kilogram chunks of meat from its victims. The dagger-shaped, serrated teeth were disproportionately long, with crowns up to 18 cm. The massive head was highly specialized for hunting prey. The muzzle was relatively narrow compared with the back of the skull, so that the eyes actually faced forward to give the animal binocular (stereoscopic) vision. Studies on the brain, nose and ear of this animal suggest that it had excellent senses of smell and hearing as well. The brain is smaller than that of a human, which is small when compared to its body size. When an animal gets larger, it does not necessarily need a bigger control centre because it has the same number of muscles, joints and organs to control. When the large size of *Tyrannosaurus* is taken into account, its brain is fairly respectable for a dinosaur.

Often called the most fearsome predator that ever lived, *Tyrannosaurus rex* has been immortalized in movies like "Jurassic Park". With a 1.5 m long skull and teeth that had crowns up to 18 cm long, this theropod was unquestionably the king of its world.

The body of *Tyrannosaurus* was massive. In order to maintain its balance and speed, it had to make a number of modifications from its smaller cousins. The neck has become shorter, and more sinuous. This has brought the head further back so that it actually sits on top of the neck, not in front of it. The arms are reduced in length, and are smaller than those of a human. However, the bones are still strong, and the arm was powerfully muscled, so it appears that they still had a function. Perhaps they were used like grappling hooks to hold onto struggling prey as the jaws did the killing, or perhaps they held onto the female of the species during mating. Many of the bones in front of the hips are shorter, and tend to be hollow and air-filled. The tail is still relatively long and heavy, and its function was to counterbalance the huge head with its massive armament of teeth. The hind legs were powerful and long. The length of the metatarsus (flat of the foot) in particular suggests that *Tyrannosaurus* and its kin were fast moving animals.

Tyrannosaurus was one of the last of the predatory dinosaurs. Its remains have been found in provinces and states throughout western North America, but the best specimens are from Alberta, Montana, South Dakota and Wyoming. Another tyrannosaurid that lived in the same region at the same time is the diminutive *Nanotyrannus*. This animal has a more primitive appearance, partly because of its small size. Tyrannosaurids, like all predatory dinosaurs, have the same number of teeth in their jaws when they are born as they do when they die. The fact that *Nanotyrannus* has an extra four teeth in its upper jaws shows that it cannot be a juvenile *Tyrannosaurus rex*.

Tyrannosaurids were the dominant theropods in both North America and Asia throughout the Late Cretaceous. *Albertosaurus* was a smaller form, up to 8 m long, that ranged from Texas to Alaska. Specimens of this animal are far more common, and it is better understood. A contemporary was the slightly more massive *Daspletosaurus*, which is currently known only from Alberta and Montana.

The metatarsal bones, which in humans make up the flat of the foot and support the toes, are long in tyrannosaurids, suggesting that these animals could move very quickly.

Left ~ Too large and bulky to catch a passing hypsilophodont, Acrocanthosaurus continues to hunt for larger prey. The high spines along its back gave this allosaurid a distinctive appearance.

In Asia, the dominant tyrannosaur was *Tarbosaurus*, a huge beast up to 12 m long. It is so much like *Tyrannosaurus* that some believe it to be simply another species of the same genus. The most primitive tyrannosaurid, *Alectrosaurus*, is found in 95 million year old rocks in China and Mongolia. It is a smaller, more gracile form with a lower, longer skull. *Alioramus* is a more enigmatic tyrannosaurid from the end of the Cretaceous; it has a low skull characterized by rough, bony protuberances on the nose.

Other specimens from other parts of the world have been assigned to the Tyrannosauridae, although most are not well enough known to be certain of the identifications. *Indosuchus* is a medium-sized form from the Upper Cretaceous of India. Although incompletely known, it has teeth at the front of the mouth that are D-shaped in cross-section (David Lambert, A Fieldguide to Dinosaurs, New York 1983). This is one of the easiest ways to identify a tyrannosaurid. A puzzling animal is *Dryptosaurus*, from the very end of the Cretaceous of New Jersey in the United States. It is known from only a partial skeleton and some isolated bones and teeth, but appears to have been a relatively large theropod that had long powerful arms to help it bring down its prey.

Tyrannosaurids were a diverse family, and included the low-skulled *Alioramus* from the Late Cretaceous of Mongolia. The bumps on the bridge of the nose probably supported a series of small horns, the function of which was probably ornamental.

Although tyrannosaurids are generally thought of as carnosaurs that evolved from allosaurids, they in fact are more closely related to small theropods like *Troodon* and *Ornithomimus*. This idea was first proposed by the eminent German palaeontologist Friedrich von Huene in 1923, but was largely ignored until the last few years when three dinosaur palaeontologists reached the same conclusion independently.

Spinosauridae

An unusual group of large carnivorous dinosaurs lived in northern Africa during the Early Cretaceous. *Spinosaurus* is a large animal, reaching a length of 12 m and a weight of more than 6 tonnes. It has a long, almost crocodile-like snout, and teeth that lack the serrated edges so characteristic of all other theropods. The spines of the vertebrae are even more unusual because they are so tall. They can be up to eleven times the length of the vertebra itself. Together they form a sail on the back of the animal that is taller than most men. The purpose of the sail is unknown, but has provoked a lot of speculation. Perhaps it was simply a display structure, used by the males to attract females, or to scare away other males with smaller sails. It is also possible that they were used as heat exchangers. By exposing them to the sun, the animals would have warmed up quickly; heat could also be lost quickly by turning away from the direct rays of the sun, especially if there was a breeze or wind. One can see that if *Spinosaurus* was a cold-blooded animal, it would have had a distinct advantage over potential prey if it could warm up more rapidly. In the morning it could start hunting while the plant-eaters were still cold and sluggish. It is more likely, however, that the sail was used simply to help dissipate heat, because *Spinosaurus* lived within the tropics. One of the large herbivores that lived in the same area, *Ouranosaurus*, also had extremely high spines on its vertebrae.

Following page ~ In the tropical forests of northern Africa, dinosaurs developed special adaptations for keeping cool. The giant Spinosaurus had greatly elongate spines along its backbone, creating a sail with extensive sheets of skin where blood vessels could dump excess heat into the atmosphere.

There are other tall-spined theropods, but none are related to *Spinosaurus*. *Acrocanthosaurus* has already been discussed, and lacks all of the other unusual

Left ~ Pivoting on its hind legs away from the charging Albertosaurus, Euoplocephalus brings its tail into play, hoping to hit the legs of the attacker.

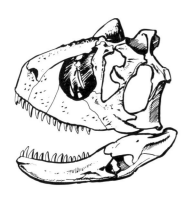

Carnotaurus had a relatively short, deep skull, with an unusual pair of horn-like processes over the eyes.

characteristics of *Spinosaurus* other than the high spines. *Altispinax* is a European genus based on nothing more than a few vertebrae. Like *Spinosaurus*, the vertebrae have extremely high spines, but other features suggest *Altispinax* is more closely related to *Megalosaurus* than *Spinosaurus*.

The skeleton of *Spinosaurus* is incompletely known, and in fact the best specimen of this animal was one of the casualties of the Second World War. The unusual characteristics of the jaws and teeth suggest it may have been a fish-eating animal that spent much of its life in the water.

Abelisauridae

During Cretaceous times, dinosaur faunas of the northern and southern hemispheres were evolving independently. Whereas tyrannosaurids dominated in the northern hemisphere, abelisaurids were the major carnivores below the equator. These large animals have fused up ankle bones, and often have bizarre characteristics in the skull. The best known abelisaurid is *Carnotaurus*, which had a short-faced skull equipped with laterally projecting horns over the eyes. The arms, like those of *Tyrannosaurus rex*, are very short and look like they would have been useless. It is difficult to evaluate the evolutionary position of abelisaurids, because they retain many primitive characteristics that suggest they separated from the main line of carnosaurian evolution even before megalosaurids had appeared.

Abelisaurids have been found mostly in Africa, India and South America, but recently have also been found in southern Europe (France, Spain and possibly Romania). It would appear that at the end of the Cretaceous African forms were invading Europe.

Segnosauridae

Although segnosaurs like *Erlikosaurus* were theropods, the skull looks more like that of a plant-eating prosauropod. The leaf-shaped teeth may have been used to kill and cut up fish.

Segnosaurs are an unusual group of dinosaurs from the Cretaceous of China, Kazakhstan, Mongolia, and possibly Canada. They are so different from other theropods that some scientists have classified them as prosauropods, ornithischians and even sauropods. Although all forms known are from the Cretaceous, they look primitive enough to be Triassic animals. The largest specimens are about 9 m long with a height of 2.4 m. They were broad, stocky animals in appearance, although they have hollow, air-filled bones like other theropods. The hips are wide, and the pubis is oriented backwards so that it superficially resembles that of an ornithischian. The skull is similar to that of a prosauropod, and has the leaf-like teeth of a herbivore. There are no teeth at the front of the jaws, however, and it is possible that this region was encased in a horny beak.

The foot of a segnosaur is unusual for a theropod in that four toes touched the ground rather than three. This appears to have been a secondary adaptation in that the short toe, which is on the back of the foot of most theropods, has become elongate and weight supporting. Although segnosaurs have blunt, leaf-like teeth and bulky bodies, the claws on the hands and feet are amazingly curved and sharp. Even tyrannosaurs did not have such ferocious claws.

A hunting Carnotaurus catches sight of a hypsilophodont carcass in the Argentine forest of 100 million years ago. Although not much more than a few mouthfuls, the carcass will ease the pain of hunger until the giant can catch something fresh. Skin impressions found in Argentina indicate that there were many large "scales" on Carnotaurus.

Segnosaurs had strongly recurved claws that would have been formidable weapons. They are deep and narrow, and terminate in sharp points. In the living animals, there would have been a continually growing epidermal sheath (like our fingernails) on the outside of the bone, lengthening it by 25 % or more.

Segnosaur specimens are found in association with river and lake sediments, and it appears that these animals may have been fish-eaters that lived along the shorelines of large bodies of water.

Alxasaurus is an Early Cretaceous segnosaur recently described from China. Other forms, including *Segnosaurus, Enigmosaurus,* and *Nanshiungosaurus* are more massive animals from the Late Cretaceous of China and Mongolia. A more gracile animal, *Erlikosaurus*, was described from Mongolia, but bones have been found in China and Canada that seem to represent either the same animal or a closely related form.

Therizinosaurids are enigmatic theropods known mostly from their front limbs and huge, weakly curved claws that can be almost a metre long. The arms are massive, but not particularly long. When the claws of this Late Cretaceous animal were first discovered in Mongolia, they were described as the bones of a gigantic turtle. The dinosaurian nature was only recognized when more claws were discovered, this time attached to arm bones. The rest of the skeleton is unknown, so the nature of the beast is completely speculative. It is possible that *Therizinosaurus* is most closely related to segnosaurs. If that is the case, it probably was not an active carnivore. The shapes of the claws are reminiscent of those of modern ant-eating mammals, and it is conceivable that therizinosaurs used their enormous claws for digging up ant hills.

Ornithomimidae

The Cretaceous was rich in habitats, which gave dinosaurs many opportunities to diversify. One of the most successful families of Late Cretaceous theropods is the Ornithomimidae (bird mimics). Their history is obscure, although unquestionable ornithomimids had appeared by the end of the Early Cretaceous. A Late Jurassic theropod, *Elaphrosaurus*, from Africa is often cited as a possible ancestor for the ornithomimids. The skull of this animal is unknown, however, and the skeleton is much more primitive. Recently, Sankar Chatterjee described the skull of a Triassic animal from Texas that he called *Shuvosaurus*. The similarity between this animal and ornithomimids is startling, but it appears to be an example of convergent evolution. An Early Cretaceous ornithomimid from Mongolia (*Harpymimus*) is quite primitive, and has the remnants of degenerated teeth in its lower jaws. This suggests that the ornithomimids had only just recently evolved in the Early Cretaceous, and could not have been around since the Triassic. *Garudimimus* is a toothless dinosaur closely related to the ornithomimids. It has a more primitive skull and foot, which is not surprising, considering that it was found in the earliest beds of Late Cretaceous age.

Ornithomimids were the ostriches of the dinosaur world. The long, thin, flexible neck supported a long head with a toothless, bird-like beak. The brain was relatively large, and the eyes were huge. Some of the ornithomimids seem to have had opposable fingers, which would have allowed them to manipulate food in their hands. The claws were almost straight, but were long and sharp. These animals could move very quickly on their long, slender legs, each of which had three functional toes with blunt, hoof-like nails. It is doubtful that there were any dinosaurs capable of outrunning an ornithomimid.

Because of their theropod ancestry, it is doubtful that ornithomimids were herbivores, although it is conceivable that they supplemented their meat diet with seeds and fruit. Their toothless mouths would also have been suited to eating smaller animals like insects, frogs, lizards and mammals, or perhaps the eggs of dinosaurs. The long legs would have helped them to catch food, but were probably more important as a means of escape from predatory relatives.

The largest of the known ornithomimids was *Gallimimus* from the Late Cretaceous of southern Mongolia. Many specimens are known, ranging in size from two to four metres. *Struthiomimus* (ostrich mimic) was the largest of the North American forms, and its remains are most commonly recovered from western North America. Smaller forms of the same region are *Ornithomimus* and *Dromiceiomimus*.

Ornithomimids appear to be closely related to other Late Cretaceous families of dinosaurs, especially the troodontids and tyrannosaurids. The evidence is based on similarities in the bones of the braincase, vertebrae and foot.

Deinocheiridae

Deinocheirus is one of the most remarkable dinosaurs discovered in recent years. It is only known from a pair of huge (2.6 m) arms discovered by one of the Polish-Mongolian expeditions to the Upper Cretaceous rocks of the Gobi Desert. The three-

Ornithomimids like *Struthiomimus* ("ostrich mimic") had amazingly bird-like heads. Although their jaws were toothless, they were closely related to theropods like troodontids and tyrannosaurids.

ORNITHOMIMIDS

Anserimimus. A fairly advanced form that is unfortunately known from only a partial skeleton. Upper Cretaceous, Mongolia.

Archaeornithomimus. Many skeletons of this animal have been found in a bonebed. Upper Cretaceous, China.

Dromiceiomimus. A fairly lightweight ornithomimid. Upper Cretaceous, Alberta, Canada.

Gallimimus. The largest ornithomimid presently known, it is represented by juvenile and adult specimens. Upper Cretaceous, Mongolia.

Ornithomimus. A gracile ornithomimid, with long, slender fingernails. Upper Cretaceous, United States and Canada.

Struthiomimus. The largest and best known of the North American ornithomimids. Upper Cretaceous, Canada and United States.

Left ~ Characteristic of the lakeside faunas of central Asia during the Cretaceous period, segnosaurs may have been fish-eaters. Although their bodies were wide and bulky, the bones were lightly built; so perhaps animals like Segnosaurus were good swimmers.

fingered hands had enormous claws measuring up to 30 cm. Several lines of evidence suggest that the deinocheirids are related to, and possibly descended from, ornithomimids.

Dromaeosauridae

Dromaeosaurids were one of the most successful families of theropods during the Late Cretaceous. In some ways, they are relatively primitive animals. Their legs, for example, are short and stocky when compared with those of ornithomimids, troodontids and tyrannosaurids. There are some very distinctive characteristics that separated dromaeosaurids from other theropods. Foremost of these is foot structure. Whereas most theropods have three toes that touch the ground, in dromaeosaurids the innermost toe has developed a huge, sickle-shaped claw that was held off the ground. The razor-sharp weapon was probably used to disembowel prey. The tail of a dromaeosaurid is stiffened by thin, flexible rods of bone, and the pubis in the hips has rotated backwards into the same position as in birds. Many other birdlike characters have led several palaeontologists to the conclusion that either dromaeosaurids are ancestral to birds, or that they are in fact flightless birds.

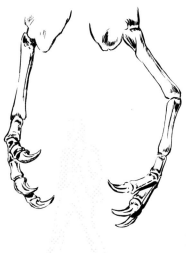

Deinocheirus is an enigmatic dinosaur known mostly from a pair of isolated arms 2.6 m long. Although clearly a theropod, its relationships are unclear. The elongate arms suggest that it may be related to the ornithomimids.

A pack of Gallimimus run in panic from the spreading flames of a forest fire. The climatic conditions of central Asia during the Late Cretaceous were generally dry, and forested belts along the rivers were susceptible to lightning strikes. But even the swift ornithomimids would have found it hard to outrun a forest fire if the winds were strong.

Most dromaeosaurids, including *Dromaeosaurus, Saurornitholestes* and *Velociraptor*, are relatively small animals, and as such are outside of the scope of this book. In 1993, however, the discovery of a new, giant form was reported from Utah. *Utahraptor* is an Early Cretaceous dromaeosaurid that would have been larger and heavier than a man. This is not the only record of giant dromaeosaurs, however. Most of a skeleton of an undescribed species was found in rocks of the same age in Mongolia, while another undescribed form has been recovered from a quarry in Japan.

One of the better known dromaeosaurids, *Deinonychus*, was found in a Lower Cretaceous quarry in Montana that produced many specimens. This evidence suggests that dromaeosaurids may have been animals that travelled in packs. If that is the case, they may have been able to kill herbivorous dinosaurs that were much larger than themselves.

Troodontidae

Troodontids were man-sized dinosaurs that have attracted a lot of attention in recent years. Whereas people have generally thought of dinosaurs as being small-brained animals, *Troodon* from the Late Cretaceous of North America has done much to change this opinion. Although its brain would not be considered large by today's standards, the mammals and birds of the Cretaceous were no better off than this dinosaur. In fact, its brain was six times the size of that of a crocodile of the same size, which puts it into the lower range of modern mammals and birds. *Troodon* inspired one Canadian scientist to extrapolate on where evolution might have taken this dinosaur if it had not become extinct. It was only a thought experiment, of course, but the resultant dinosauroid attracted a lot of attention internationally, and made the point that dinosaurs were evolving into larger brained forms. That trend is not unique to mammals.

Dromaeosaurus was a small but powerfully built theropod from Late Cretaceous times. Like its cousin *Velociraptor*, it has one enlarged sickle-claw on each foot.

Troodontids had long hind limbs, each armed with an enlarged raptorial claw held off the ground like that of a dromaeosaurid. There are many differences between troodontids and dromaeosaurids, however, so it is unlikely that they are closely related. The tail lacks the stiffening rods of bone that are found in dromaeosaurids, and the legs indicate that troodontids were much faster runners. The skulls have large, forward facing eyes, showing these animals had stereoscopic vision, and may have been able to see well after dark. The teeth are relatively small and numerous, but have huge serrations. The long arms end in fingers that were well suited for handling small objects. It would appear that troodontids may have hunted mammals, lizards and other small animals.

Troodontids are known only from the Cretaceous of the northern hemisphere at present. Some teeth from Upper Jurassic rocks of Dinosaur National Monument in Utah may be from a troodontid. Other forms include *Sinornithoides*, a chicken-sized form from the Early Cretaceous of China, and *Saurornithoides*, a man-sized, Late Cretaceous troodontid from China and Mongolia. Other species are known from Europe, although the specimens are very incomplete. The best of these is *Bradycneme* found in the terminal Cretaceous rocks of Romania.

DROMAEOSAURIDS

Adasaurus. A relatively poorly known animal, although good specimens have been collected. Upper Cretaceous, Mongolia.

Deinonychus. Discovered in the 1960s, this animal was instrumental in the development of physiological studies on dinosaurs. Lower Cretaceous, Montana, U.S.A.

Dromaeosaurus. The first dromaeosaurid described, but one of the rarest. Upper Cretaceous, Alberta, Canada.

Saurornitholestes. A North American version of *Velociraptor*. Upper Cretaceous, Alberta, Canada.

Utahraptor. The largest dromaeosaurid presently described, although specimens at least as large have been found in Mongolia and Japan. Lower Cretaceous, Utah, U.S.A.

Velociraptor. A small but widespread form, *Velociraptor* teeth have been found in Europe. Upper Cretaceous, China and Mongolia.

Velociraptor was probably an opportunist that would generally hunt prey smaller than itself, such as the Cretaceous lizard Macrocephalosaurus, or would collect into packs to go after larger prey.

In many ways, troodontids are the most birdlike of the theropods, and it is quite possible that they are the closest relatives of true birds. The presence of an enlarged raptorial claw on each foot is one character that shows troodontids could not have been directly ancestral to birds, however.

Other Theropods

Theropods during the Cretaceous were as diverse as modern carnivores. Several other families had bizarre, highly specialized forms that are worth noting. Oviraptorids are in many ways the most peculiar forms. The original specimen found in Mongolia in 1923 was found on a nest of eggs that were identified as *Protoceratops*. It was assumed that the theropod, which had toothless jaws ideally suited for crushing eggs, was probably eating the eggs when it was buried by a sudden sand storm. Eggs can only be identified when they have embryonic material associated with them, however. The discovery by a Sino-Canadian expedition of a second specimen of *Oviraptor* on a nest of the same type of eggs suggests that this dinosaur may have been much maligned. The new specimen was squatting over the eggs, and it now appears more likely that both specimens were simply protecting their own nests. Two other oviraptorids, *Ingenia* and *Conchoraptor*, are known from the Late Cretaceous of Mongolia. Closely related, toothless forms were discovered in rocks of the same age in North America. These animals, known as caenagnathids, were long thought to have been birds. In addition to *Caenagnathus* from Alberta, a large, undescribed form was recently found in the latest Cretaceous beds of South Dakota and Saskatchewan, and parts of a very small species were discovered in Kazakhstan. At present, caenagnathids are only known from isolated bones from the skull and lower jaws.

There were many small theropods in the Cretaceous, including toothless forms like *Oviraptor*. This strange little dinosaur had a crest over the snout.

Elmisaurids are known from both Asia and North America, although no specimen has ever been found with a skull. The recovery of both caenagnathids and elmisaurids from the same rocks suggests that they may in fact be the same thing. Unfortunately, this problem will not be resolved until a skeleton with a skull is found. Hopes for this were raised recently when a skeleton found in Alberta in the 1920s was finally uncrated for preparation in the 1990s. At the time of writing, it is still not known whether or not the skeleton has an associated skull.

ORNITHISCHIA

The bird-hipped dinosaurs are far more common in the Cretaceous than saurischians. Although they never attained the dimensions of some of the sauropods, some species weighed more than bull elephants. Over time, they evolved into many diverse lines. All were herbivores that had the bird-hipped pubic bone, with both anterior and posterior processes. Primitively, the teeth of ornithischians were leaf-shaped, but relatively simple. Later species developed massive banks of closely-packed, fast-growing teeth. As the teeth wore down they formed rough surfaces for chopping or grinding plants as efficiently as any modern mammal. Ornithischians also developed cheek pouches so that the vegetation being processed by the teeth would not fall out of the mouth. Stiff bony rods ran along the backbones of most ornithischians in the hips and tail. These would help stiffen the tail so that it could be held high off the ground with little effort.

Following page ~ Around the middle of the Cretaceous period, the first tyrannosaurids appeared in central Asia. Alectrosaurus was more lightly built than later forms like Albertosaurus and Tyrannosaurus, but appears to have been better proportioned for running down a hypsilophodont.

Hadrosaurs have very complex dental batteries, and the teeth are closely packed together. Up to four teeth were stacked on top of each other, and as the top ones wore down from grinding tough plants, new ones replaced them from below.

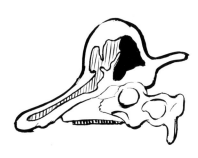

The crest of a lambeosaurine hadrosaur enclosed the nasal passages (between the nose and the throat), and a hollow chamber. The most plausible function for this arrangement is to modify and amplify sounds produced in the throat. Crests of different hadrosaur species have different shapes and proportions, which would have produced different sounds in the enclosed resonating chambers.

surprising that there is a lot of evidence to suggest they had complex behaviour.

There are two lines of recognized hadrosaurs — the hadrosaurines, which usually have flat skulls that are unornamented, and the lambeosaurines, which have characteristic hollow crests on top of the head. At one time it was thought that because duckbilled dinosaurs had a duck-like bill and webbed feet they must have spent most of their time in the water. Although some probably did follow this kind of a life-style, they were diverse enough to inhabit virtually any environment open to herbivores, including semi-arid regions that were almost deserts.

Hadrosaur nostrils are large, and connected internally to the throat so they could breathe even when chewing their food. In the lambeosaurines, the nasal passages entered a hollow chamber in the crest before continuing into the throat. The orbit was large and circular, and there were bony plates inside the eye that formed the sclerotic ring functioning like a protective apparatus of the eye. (This is typical for most reptiles and birds.). The ear had a tiny, delicate bone known as the stapes, and apparently hadrosaurs had a good sense of hearing.

The tooth batteries are quite remarkable. Each tooth is interlocked with its neighbours, and as many as four teeth are stacked into a column. As teeth were worn down by grinding vegetation, new ones would push up from below the gums and take their place. Counting the replacement teeth, there were more than 1,000 teeth in the mouth of a big hadrosaurine.

Most hadrosaurs are 8 to 10 m long. The thumb was lost from the hand, and the outer finger was reduced in size. The remaining three fingers were encased in a mitten of skin, and formed a crescent-shaped hand that left very distinctive handprints in the mud. These handprints would have been very difficult to interpret if it were not for the discovery of several natural casts of mummies. The best mummified hand is on a dinosaur collected in Wyoming, but on display at the Senckenberg Museum of Natural History in Frankfurt. Hadrosaurs had long hind legs with three toes that ended in blunt, hoof-like nails. Like iguanodontids, they had huge pads of soft tissue under each toe and the heel.

The fossilized impressions of hadrosaur skin are found sometimes in North America and Asia. These are usually associated with skeletons that were buried rapidly, but sometimes the impressions are in the bottoms of well-preserved footprints. In general, the skin was composed of a mosaic of tiny bumps that do not really qualify as scales. Sometimes, as in the case of *Saurolophus* from Mongolia, there are large, wide tubercles surrounded by small ones. These rosette patterns in the skin suggest that there may have been corresponding colour patterns. The tail of at least one type of hadrosaurine (*Edmontosaurus*) had tall, blade-like scales on top. Although hadrosaur skin is usually preserved only as impressions in the Cretaceous mud, one specimen from New Mexico is fossilized skin, and the epidermal and dermal layers can be seen under a microscope.

The lambeosaurines had a variety of different crest shapes that characterize individual species. *Corythosaurus* (helmeted reptile) had a relatively simple but prominent crest, *Lambeosaurus* had a double crest, and *Parasaurolophus* had a

Right ~ An ominous shadow startles a hadrosaur into action. The Brachylophosaurus has been caught too far from the herd, and unless something unexpected happens, it is unlikely to escape the larger, faster tyrannosaur.

long tubular process that doubled the length of the head. These and other hadrosaurs co-existed in the Late Cretaceous of Alberta. It is possible that the crests were one way that the hadrosaurs could tell each other apart visually. Because they are hollow and connected to the nasal passages, it is also highly likely that they were used as resonating chambers. By having different shapes, the different lambeosaurines would actually sound different from each other, and this is another way that one individual could recognize another of the same species. Baby lambeosaurines did not have high crests, which only developed when the animals were almost full grown and presumably sexually mature. That is when it would have been important to identify each other.

Hadrosaurs appeared at the end of the Early Cretaceous in the northern hemisphere, and survived until the very end of the Cretaceous. Their fossils are common in North America, South America, Europe and Asia.

How Hadrosaurs Lived

Because hadrosaur fossils are so common in the Late Cretaceous, we probably know more about their life styles than we do about any other dinosaur.

Footprint sites and bonebeds (massive accumulations of many animals) show that many species of hadrosaurs travelled in herds. Some of these herds were enormous, and a bonebed in Montana contains the remains of more than 10,000 individuals that appear to have died en masse in a volcanic ash fall. Palaeontologists have asked themselves why so many large animals, each weighing up to 4 tonnes, would gather together into such massive herds. The herds would have caused tremendous damage to any ecosystem, so it is unlikely that they stayed in one place for very long. The discovery of hadrosaur bonebeds within the Arctic Circle suggests one reason that they may have been herding. During the summer months the arctic would have been highly productive in plants because the sun would have been shining up to 24 hours a day. Hadrosaurs, to take advantage of this rich and abundant source of food, would gather into herds in spring and push north into the Arctic Circle. There they would disperse until autumn, when the approaching period of complete darkness would cause most plants to become dormant for winter. It was not too cold at that time, but there would not have been enough food. So the hadrosaurs would gather into herds again, and push south to regions where they could get food during winter. The long migrations may have occupied up to four months of the annual cycle, but were feasible because these animals had long legs and were efficient walkers.

Nesting sites in Montana and Alberta show that some species of hadrosaurs (both hadrosaurines and lambeosaurines) herded when they were laying eggs. The nesting colonies could be protected better against the attacks of carnivores by the adult hadrosaurs, although the chances of survival were not as good at the edge of the colony. The nests appear to have been 2 m wide depressions scooped in the sand or dirt. They were separated by 4 or 5 m, so there was ample room for the adults to move between them. A nest contained up to thirty eggs, each of which had a diameter of about 20 cm. Although this is small for such large animals, larger eggs would have required thicker shells to support themselves. And if the shells were too thick, not enough air would get

HADROSAURS
(LATE CRETACEOUS)

Anatotion
Canada, United States

Aralosaurus
Kazakhstan

Bactrosaurus
China

Barsboldia
Mongolia

Brachylophosaurus
Canada, United States

Claosaurus
United States

Corythosaurus
Canada

Edmontosaurus
Canada, United States

Gilmoreosaurus
China

Gryposaurus
Canada, United States

Hadrosaurus
United States

Hypacrosaurus
Canada, United States

Jaxartosaurus
Kazakhstan, China

Kritosaurus
United States

Lambeosaurus
Canada, Mexico

Lophorhothon
United States

Maiasaura
Canada, United States

Mandschurosaurus
China, Russia

Nipponosaurus
Russia

Parasaurolophus
Canada, United States

Prosaurolophus
Canada, United States

Saurolophus
Canada, Mongolia

Secernosaurus
Argentina

Shantungosaurus
China

Tanius
China

Telmatosaurus
France, Romania, Spain

Tsintaosaurus
China

Left ~ Two young hadrosaurs hide beneath their mother when they are startled by a sound in the forest. Corythosaurus babies have relatively low crests compared to the magnificent crests of the adults.

As the eggs hatch, Hypacrosaurus lies protectively beside the nest. Because of the great disparity in size between babies and adults, hatchlings may have been restricted to the nest for the first few months of their lives so as not to be stepped on by the adults. Adults would have brought

them food, possibly regurgitating partly digested plants. In this way the babies would have acquired the necessary microbes in the digestive tract for the digestion of plants. Embryos already had worn teeth, showing that they ground their teeth together inside the eggs so they would be functional at birth.

through to the developing babies. Furthermore, the babies would not have had the strength to break the shells when they were ready to hatch. A baby *Maiasaura* was only half a metre long when it hatched from the egg. Evidence suggests that they remained in the nest for as much as a couple of months. During that time, one or both of the parents brought food to the nest. The babies grew rapidly, and within months had increased their body size to the point that they could travel with the herd. The high growth rate in hadrosaurs is one line of evidence used to suggest that these animals might have been warm-blooded, at least when they were babies.

At present we know of 18 species of hadrosaurines and 14 species of lambeosaurines. *Edmontosaurus* is one of the last hadrosaurines, and one of the largest, reaching a length of more than 11 m. It was first discovered in Alberta, but is now recorded from Colorado in the south to Alaska in the north. Recent discoveries in Siberia suggest that it crossed an ancient land connection into Asia. Another large hadrosaurine, *Saurolophus*, is characterized by a solid spike-like crest on top of its head. Species of this dinosaur are known in both Alberta and Mongolia. The Mongolian species of *Saurolophus* is enormous, about 15 m long. Another hadrosaurine, *Shantungosaurus*, is about the same size, but is from eastern China. *Tsintaosaurus* has a solid crest, but still appears to have been a hadrosaurine. According to some workers, the crest is simply the nasal bones reorientated by crushing after the animal died. This mystery will be solved only when the specimen has been and examined in more detail. The best known European hadrosaur is *Telmatosaurus* from the Carpathian Mountains of Romania.

There is considerable debate as to whether *Tsintaosaurus* had a peculiar, spikelike crest of solid bone, or whether this supposed crest is a bone that normally lies flat along the top of the skull.

The crest of *Saurolophus* is solid, which is one reason that this dinosaur is considered to be one of the hadrosaurine (flat-headed) hadrosaurs, rather than one of the crested lambeosaurines. *Saurolophus* specimens have been discovered in both Alberta and Mongolia.

Lambeosaurines include several species of *Parasaurolophus*, each with the strange, tubular crest enclosing the convoluted narial passages. The more common *Corythosaurus* and *Lambeosaurus* were each about 10 m long at maturity. *Hypacrosaurus* was a closely related form that had two species. *Hypacrosaurus altispinus* is characterized by high spines on its vertebrae. The other species has just been described, and is based on embryos, babies and adults from Alberta and Montana. There are many poorly known lambeosaurines from other parts of the world, including *Barsboldia* from Mongolia, *Nipponosaurus* from Sakhalin Island (Russia), and *Jaxartosaurus* from Kazakhstan and China. Unfortunately, the most distinctive anatomical character of a lambeosaurine, the crest, is unknown in each of these last three genera. The situation is more confusing with *Mandschurosaurus*, which was excavated from the Amur River between China and Russia. The original specimen, mounted in St. Petersburg, is a composite skeleton that includes both hadrosaurine and lambeosaurine bones.

Pachycephalosauridae

Pachycephalosaurs ("thick-headed reptiles") are Cretaceous ornithischians characterized by the thick bones on top of the skull. In many pachycephalosaur species, the bone forms a dome that gives the animal a high skull and the appearance of being intelligent. However, the brain cavity is much thinner than the thickness of the bone. It has been proposed that the skull thickening allowed the males to butt heads the same way that mountain sheep do today. However, the skull roof is solid, and if a pachycephalosaurid hit anything solid, there was no mechanism to protect the brain from the vibrations that would have passed through the bone.

Right ~ A family of Lambeosaurus cautiously bend to drink water in the early morning light. Should any danger appear, at least one of the group should catch sight of it and warn the others with a loud honk.

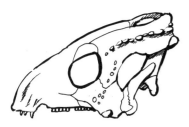

Some pachycephalosaurids did not have domed skulls. Although the skull roof was thick, it was flat on top, like that of *Homalocephale*.

Below ~ From a vantage point high on a hill, Homalocephale watches for the approach of danger. The shape of the skull, flat on top, helped distinguish it from other pachycephalosaurids.

In modern mammals that butt heads, there are huge sinuses (air cavities) in the skull to absorb the shock. Horns on the back of the skull of *Stygimoloch* would also have interfered with head butting. So it may be that the thickened skulls of pachycephalosaurs were used to either hit softer targets (the body of a predator or a rival pachycephalosaur), or were simply used as ornamentation to simplify identification.

In species that are well known, it is apparent that there are two types of domes. The specimens with thicker, higher domes are generally assumed to be males. The fact that there are differences between the domes of males and females supports the idea that the domes were used at least in part as visual stimuli for other members of their own species. This is not surprising, because we know that pachycephalosaurs and other dinosaurs were highly visual animals.

The head on a pachycephalosaur was relatively heavy. To maintain its balance, the head needed to be pulled closer to the hips. Therefore the neck of a pachycephalosaur (cervicals are not known) was rather sinuous, and the attachment for the skull was vertical (as in humans) rather than horizontal (as in most animals). The tail is relatively heavy and is stiffened by ossified tendons as in most other ornithischians. Pachycephalosaurs had relatively short legs, and probably were not capable of running very fast.

The teeth are leaf-like in shape, and quite primitive for an ornithischian. Presumably they did not eat the tough leaves and twigs that hadrosaurs were able to process, but they probably did have a varied, herbaceous diet.

Pachycephalosaurs were a diverse and widespread group of dinosaurs, but they are rather poorly known because skeletons are rarely found. This suggests that they lived in habitats where the chances of being fossilized were not particularly good. Because the skull caps are made of such thick bone. they do tend to be found much more frequently.

Fifteen genera of pachycephalosaurs are presently recognized. Most are from North America and Asia, but specimens have also been found on the Isle of Wight and Madagascar. The majority were relatively small animals, but *Pachycephalosaurus* from the Late Cretaceous of North America was as large as a hadrosaur. Although a complete skeleton of this animal has never been found, its length can be estimated at 8 m. Its massive dome was 25 cm thick, and it had short bony spikes on its nose and at the back of the skull.

Pachycephalosaurids generally had high, domelike skulls that made them look as though they were intelligent, large-brained animals. However, most of the dome was composed of solid bone, and the brain was actually quite small.

Above ~ Shantungosaurus was an enormous hadrosaur from the province of Shandong in eastern China. In appearance, it is similar to flat-headed hadrosaurs from North America.

121

Stygimoloch was one of the larger, more ornamental pachycephalosaurs. The horns on the back of the skull were probably mostly used for display. The largest animals would have had relatively larger spikes, and presumably large males could intimidate potential competitors by their appearance. But when rival males fought for the

attention of a harem, they may have used the thick skulls and horns to ram each other's sides. Because the dome is solid bone, there is no cushioning for the brain if the head struck anything hard. It is therefore unlikely that pachycephalosaurids rammed their heads together the way mountain sheep do.

The teeth of pachycephalosaurids are simple, primitive and relatively small, and offer few clues as to what kind of plants these dinosaurs ate.

PACHYCEPHALOSAURS

Goyocephale
  Mongolia

Gravitholus
  Canada

Homalocephale
  Mongolia

Majungatholus
  Madagascar

Micropachycephalosaurus
  China

Ornatotholus
  Canada

Pachycephalosaurus
  Canada, United States

Prenocephale
  Mongolia

Stegoceras
  Canada, United States

Stygimoloch
  United States

Tylocephale
  Mongolia

Wannanosaurus
  China

Yaverlandia
  England

The most commonly found pachycephalosaur fossils belong to a 2 m long animal from Alberta. *Stegoceras* is known from only one reasonably good skeleton with a complete skull, but more than a hundred domes have been collected. *Prenocephale* (Mongolia) and *Gravitholus* (Alberta) are similar animals, except that the domes are much fuller. At the other end of the scale, *Homalocephale* (Mongolia) and *Ornatotholus* (Alberta) had thick skulls, but not thick enough to form domes. The earliest known form is *Yaverlandia* from the Lower Cretaceous rocks of the Isle of Wight in Britain. A partial skull of a pachycephalosaurid, *Majungatholus*, was found in the Upper Cretaceous of Madagascar, and so far is the only record from the southern hemisphere.

Stegosauria

Stegosaurs survived into the Cretaceous in several parts of the world, although they clearly were not as common as they had been during Jurassic times. *Craterosaurus* is based on an incomplete vertebra from the Lower Cretaceous of England, whereas a partial skull (*Paranthodon*) shows that stegosaurs were living around the same time in South Africa. Again, China has provided much better material in recent years. *Wuerhosaurus*'s skeletons have been found in Lower Cretaceous rocks from Xinjiang in northwestern China, and from Inner Mongolia. These animals were about 7 m long, and have long, low plates of bone. One stegosaur has been reported from the Late Cretaceous

of southern India. However, *Dravidosaurus* is based on rather fragmentary material, and many suspect that the identification as a stegosaur is incorrect. Only the discovery of better specimens will determine whether or not stegosaurs survived into Late Cretaceous times.

Ankylosauria

Although ankylosaurs are armoured thyreophorans like stegosaurs, they are very different types of animals. Whereas stegosaurs dominated the Late Jurassic and dwindled during the Cretaceous, ankylosaurs had their beginnings in the early Late Jurassic, and prospered throughout the Cretaceous. All ankylosaurs have rather low, broad bodies that are covered by a mosaic of bony plates embedded in the skin. These plates sometimes fused together to form larger, more solid masses, but usually remained separate. The short, broad skull was also armoured, and the bony plates fused to the skull bones. Smaller bony plates helped to protect the cheeks, the throat, and in some forms even the eyelids. The teeth were relatively small, and leaf-like. It is hard to understand what kinds of plants they could have been chewing because they seem so inadequate for such massive bodies. It has been suggested that these animals may have been ant-eaters, like some of the modern armoured mammals. However, there is no strong evidence to support this theory. Both arms and legs were relatively short, but powerful. The smallest ankylosaurs were only a few metres long, whereas the largest were about 8 m.

Sauropelta, one of the few ankylosaurs from North America with reasonably well-preserved skeletons, would have looked formidable with its large, forward-facing spikes along the neck and shoulder.

The Ankylosauria actually includes two distinct families, the Nodosauridae and the Ankylosauridae, which seem to have had long, independent histories.

Nodosaurids tend to be more lightly built, and have a much wider geographic distribution. They have been discovered in Antarctica, Australia, Europe and North America, and are likely to be found eventually in Africa and South America. Their absence from the rocks of Asia is a mystery.

The skull of a nodosaurid tends to have a longer, narrower snout than an ankylosaurid. The legs are also longer, suggesting that these were more agile animals. Nodosaurids have large spikes projecting outwards from the base of the neck and the shoulders. They do not have a club at the end of the tail. *Polacanthus* from the Early Cretaceous of England is one of the better known genera, thanks to better material found recently on the Isle of Wight. A closely related nodosaurid, which has not yet been named, was found recently in beds of the same age in eastern Utah. In these animals, the small bony plates fuse together over the hips to form a protective shell that lacks the flexibility of the rest of the armour. *Sauropelta* is a larger animal from the Lower Cretaceous rocks of Montana, Utah and Wyoming. Up to 7.5 m in length, *Sauropelta* probably weighed several tonnes with its armour. The Late Cretaceous nodosaurids of western North America were about the same length, but were more massive and more heavily armoured. *Edmontonia* and *Panoplosaurus* are known from numerous skulls and partial skeletons. An almost complete skeleton, with armour, of a small nodosaurid called *Minmi* was found recently in Australia. Palaeontologists are anxiously awaiting the description of this new form to see how it relates to species in the northern hemisphere.

The crown of an ankylosaur tooth is smaller than your finger-nail, although it has a long root to anchor it in the jaw. The ridges on a tooth of *Edmontonia* helped chop up vegetation by providing serrations along the margin of the tooth.

Left ~ Pachycephalosaurus was the largest of the dome-heads, and one of the last. As large as some of the hadrosaurs, its fossils are rare, suggesting that it may have inhabited drier regions back from the North American coastlines.

NODOSAURID ANKYLOSAURS

Acanthopholis. Early Cretaceous. England.

Denversaurus. Late Cretaceous. United States.

Edmontonia. Late Cretaceous. Canada, United States.

Hoplitosaurus. Early Cretaceous. United States.

Hylaeosaurus. Early Cretaceous. England, France.

Minmi. Early Cretaceous. Australia.

Nodosaurus. Late Cretaceous. United States.

Panoplosaurus. Late Cretaceous. Canada.

Polacanthus. Early Cretaceous. England, United States.

Sarcolestes. Middle Jurassic. England.

Sauropelta. Early Cretaceous. United States.

Silvisaurus. Early Cretaceous. United States.

"Struthiosaurus". Late Cretaceous. Romania.

Two closely related ankylosaurids, Tarchia from Mongolia (above left) and Ankylosaurus from North America (above) were huge, heavy animals. Because of the great weight of their armour, they would have had great difficulty in swimming because they would have had a tendency to roll over onto their backs and sink.

Sarcolestes is an ankylosaur found more than a century ago in Middle Jurassic beds in southern England. Unfortunately, the specimen consists only of part of a lower jaw, and this early record does not give much information about the origin of ankylosaurs. A new Jurassic ankylosaur has been discovered in northwestern China, however. The specimen, which includes part of a skull, most of the vertebral column, some of the limb bones and many of the armour plates, will be described and named in the near future.

The second family of ankylosaurs, the ankylosaurids, are generally larger and more massive than nodosaurids. The heads are short and wide, and tend to have sharp, squared-off edges at the back. The teeth are much smaller than those of nodosaurids, but have the same primitive leaf-like structure. There were no large spikes over the shoulder, but ankylosaurs did carry huge clubs of bone at the end of the tail. The armour plates on the back are hollowed out at the base, and are not as massive as those of nodosaurids.

Ankylosaurids are presently known only from the Cretaceous of North America and Asia. *Shamosaurus* is presently the oldest known ankylosaurid, and comes from the Lower Cretaceous rocks of southern Mongolia. The largest ankylosaurid, and the last, was *Ankylosaurus* from the Late Cretaceous of Alberta, Montana and Wyoming. A smaller cousin, *Euoplocephalus* is a much better known animal from the same region, although it lived a little earlier in time. In Asia, ankylosaurs seem to have been more common and more diverse. However, this may be because of differences in the environments. Asia was much drier than North America in the Late Cretaceous, and because of their heavy armour, ankylosaurs tended to avoid areas where there were lots of rivers and lakes. *Pinacosaurus* is the most common ankylosaur from China and Mongolia. It was a relatively small form, reaching a maximum length of 5 m. Twelve babies, each 1.5 m, were found in a single quarry in China by a Sino-Canadian expedition in 1988. It appears that they had probably hatched from the same nest, and had remained together as a family group until the unfortunate day when they were buried behind a sand dune during a sandstorm. The baby ankylosaurs had two half rings of armour to protect their necks, but the rest of the armour, including the tail club, had not developed by the time they died. *Saichania* and *Tarchia* were two large ankylosaurids from the Upper Cretaceous of Mongolia. They have more angular skulls than *Pinacosaurus*, and in that sense look more like North American forms.

Ceratopsia ~ the Horned Dinosaurs

The last dinosaurs to appear were the ceratopsians, or horned dinosaurs. They were advanced herbivores on a par with hadrosaurs in terms of sophistication of food processing. Although they became diverse in North America and Asia in the Late Cretaceous, their fossil record in other parts of the world is poor.

Ceratopsians are characterized in part by their enormous heads. The skull of one specimen of *Torosaurus* is 3 m in length, making up a third of the body length. Almost half of this length is the elongate frill, composed of bones from the back of the skull that extended backwards over the neck. Advanced ceratopsians also have characteristic

Right ~ Panoplosaurus, like other nodosaurid ankylosaurs, was protected by enlarged spikes in the shoulder region, but never possessed a tail club.

ANKYLOSAURID ANKYLOSAURS

Amtosaurus. Late Cretaceous. Mongolia.

Ankylosaurus. Late Cretaceous. Canada, United States.

Euoplocephalus. Late Cretaceous. Canada, United States.

Gobisaurus. Late Cretaceous, China.

Maleevus. Late Cretaceous. Mongolia.

Pinacosaurus. Late Cretaceous. China, Mongolia.

Saichania. Late Cretaceous. Mongolia.

Shamosaurus. Early Cretaceous. Mongolia.

Talarurus. Late Cretaceous. China, Mongolia.

Tarchia. Late Cretaceous. Mongolia.

Tienchisaurus. Late Jurassic. China.

The skull of *Pinacosaurus* is broader than it is long, and has rather strange looking, down-turned eyes that cannot be seen from above. Like other ankylosaurs, there is a mosaic of bony plates fused onto the outside of the skull.

Pinacosaurus babies, lacking the protective armour and tail clubs of the adults, seek protection by staying close to one of their parents. A remarkable find in China has shown that the babies remained together as a family unit when they left the nest.

Ankylosaurs like *Euoplocephalus* are very broad animals, especially across the hips. This suggests that there may have been extensive chambers along the digestive tract for the storage of food being broken down by microbial action.

The end of the tail of an adult ankylosaurid usually terminated in a heavy mass of bone formed by the fusion of bony plates in the skin.

There are four families of ceratopsians currently recognized. Psittacosaurids were small, primitive forms from the Early Cretaceous of Asia, and protoceratopsids were generally small animals from North America and Asia. The great horned ceratopsians are classified as either chasmosaurines or centrosaurines.

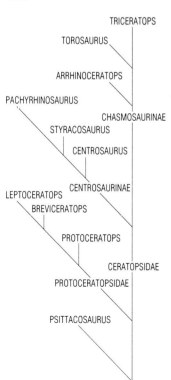

TRICERATOPS
TOROSAURUS
ARRHINOCERATOPS
PACHYRHINOSAURUS
CHASMOSAURINAE
STYRACOSAURUS
CENTROSAURUS
CENTROSAURINAE
LEPTOCERATOPS
BREVICERATOPS
PROTOCERATOPS
CERATOPSIDAE
PROTOCERATOPSIDAE
PSITTACOSAURUS

horns on their face. *Triceratops*, for example, means "three-horned face", referring to the presence of a horn on the nose and a horn over each eye. Elongation of the skull was in part a function of adaptations in the jaws for feeding. The teeth, like those of hadrosaurs, were closely packed together to form continuous grinding surfaces. The jaws also had powerful jaw muscles.

All ceratopsians have a new bone at the front of the upper jaws. It is called a rostral bone, and forms the front of the upper beak. The skull is always narrow at the front, and the beak is sharp when compared with those of other ornithischians. The cheek bone (jugal) flares out from the side of the skull, and in some advanced forms can actually bear a horn. In even the most primitive ceratopsians, there is a frill extending from the top of the skull over the attachments of the neck musculature to the skull. The roof of the mouth is highly vaulted near the front. The earliest known forms are from the Early Cretaceous.

The Ceratopsia includes psittacosaurids, protoceratopsids, and ceratopsids, representing three evolutionary grades. The most primitive level, the Psittacosauridae, were classified as ornithopods until recently.

Psittacosauridae

One of the most characteristic dinosaurs of the Lower Cretaceous rocks of central Asia is *Psittacosaurus*. More than half a dozen species, and hundreds of specimens, are recognized for this genus, but all have the same fundamental body plan. They were relatively small dinosaurs, and no specimens have been recovered that are more than 2 m long. Although they did not have horns, the back of the skull is expanded, and has extended backwards somewhat over the neck to increase the length of the jaw muscles. The cheeks are flared, and the beak is deep and narrow like that of a parrot (*Psittacosaurus* means "parrot reptile"). The hind legs were longer than the arms, but the animals probably spent most of their time walking on all fours.

A skeleton without a skull from the lowermost Cretaceous of Germany was given the name *Stenopelix*. Although this animal has been assigned at various times to either the Psittacosauridae and the Pachycephalosauridae, its taxonomic position cannot be determined with certainty until a skull is found.

Protoceratopsidae

Protoceratopsids are generally smaller than the larger horned dinosaurs that characterize the Late Cretaceous of North America. However, they can become fairly large, and an animal called *Udanoceratops* from Mongolia and China has a skull almost a metre in length, or was about four metres long. Although less specialized than the ceratopsids, protoceratopsids still survived until the end of the Cretaceous.

Like the ceratopsids, protoceratopsids have sharply pointed beaks and pronounced frills at the back of the skulls. They do not have huge horns, but many of them do have a sharp, short horn between the eyes and the nose. Each tooth has a prominent ridge, and the crowns are oval when viewed from the side. The first three vertebrae in the neck fuse together to help support the large head.

Opposite page ~ Wallowing in the mud at the edge of a stream, Anchiceratops listens carefully for the sound of any approaching danger. The juveniles have only small horns and crests, features that they will not require until they become sexually mature.

CENTROSAURINE CERATOPSIDS

Avaceratops. A small animal described by Peter Dodson in 1986. Montana.

Centrosaurus. This genus may include specimens formerly described as *Monoclonius*. One large horn over the nose, and two forward curving spikes on the back of the frill characterize this animal. Alberta, Montana.

Pachyrhinosaurus. The horn over the nose has been replaced by a massive boss of bone, which in some individuals incorporates smaller bosses over the eyes. There are characteristic spikes on the frill. Alberta, Alaska.

Styracosaurus. Centrosaurines once called *Brachyceratops* may be juvenile specimens of *Styracosaurus*. The adults have a huge horn on the nose, and an assortment of spikes at the back of the frill.

Turanoceratops. The first unquestionable ceratopsid discovered in Asia was only described in 1989. Kazakhstan.

One of the most remarkable ceratopsians is Pachyrhinosaurus, presently known from many specimens from Alberta and Alaska. The bony horn over the nose had become a massive boss of bone, which may have been

CHASMOSAURINE CERATOPSIDS

Anchiceratops has a thick frill with a distinctive pair of knobs at the back. Alberta.

Arrhinoceratops. Two large horns over the eyes and a small horn over the nose are similar to the arrangement in *Triceratops*, but the frill is larger and more open. Alberta.

Chasmosaurus has a large, squared-off frill. Most specimens have large horns over the eyes, but several skulls, which might be from females, have only short orbital horns. Alberta, Texas.

Pentaceratops means "five-horn face". There is a horn on the nose, one over each eye, and one on each cheek. New Mexico.

Torosaurus is one of the last dinosaurs, and one of the largest ceratopsians. Western North America.

Triceratops. The most famous horned dinosaur. The frill on this ceratopsian is relatively short, but lacks the openings characteristic of most other ceratopsians.

used to support a keratinous horn of unknown shape and dimensions. Large hooked spikes at the back of the frill, and additional horns in the middle of the skull behind the eyes complete the bizarre appearance.

PROTOCERATOPSIDS
(LATE CRETACEOUS)

Asiaceratops is a new form recently described from Kazakhstan.

Bagaceratops. Juveniles to adults known from Mongolia.

Breviceratops. Similar to *Protoceratops* but with a shorter face. Mongolia.

Leptoceratops. The last surviving protoceratopsian presently known. Alberta, Montana, Wyoming.

Microceratops. A small and poorly understood protoceratopsian from China and Mongolia.

Montanoceratops was, as the name suggests, originally found in Montana. One specimen is presently known from Alberta.

Protoceratops is one of the best known dinosaurs because so many specimens, from eggs and embryos to adults, have been discovered in China and Mongolia.

Udanoceratops is the largest protoceratopsian, and probably reached a length of 3 m. China, Mongolia.

Triceratops was one of the largest and last of the ceratopsians. The three horns on the face, and the relatively short frill make up one of the simplest arrangements for a horned dinosaur skull.

Protoceratops was first discovered in Mongolia in 1923 by a famous expedition of the American Museum of Natural History. The site where the specimens were found is called Bayn Dzak, and over the years several hundred skulls and skeletons have been found there. The specimens include nests of eggs, newly hatched babies, juveniles, and adults (both males and females), and *Protoceratops* is unquestionably one of the best known dinosaurs. It grew to a maximum length of 2.4 m, and what are thought to be males had small sharp horns on their noses. In larger individuals, there was a well developed frill extending up and over the neck.

Other protoceratopsians are known from Upper Cretaceous rocks of North America and Asia. One of the earliest forms was *Montanoceratops*, from Montana and Alberta. This is a relatively large, advanced form. The curious thing is that one of the most primitive protoceratopsian is *Leptoceratops*, the last known genus and a contemporary of *Triceratops*. It had a very short frill, and a rather lightly built body. *Bagaceratops* and *Breviceratops* are two more types found in the Gobi Desert. The smallest protoceratopsian is appropriately called *Microceratops*, but is known from only two incomplete specimens from Mongolia and China.

Ceratopsidae

Characterized by large skulls, prominent frills, various combinations of horns over the eyes and nose, enlarged nostrils, extra bones fused to the edges of the frill, a ball-like attachment between the skull and the neck, two-rooted teeth, fusion of ten vertebrae into the hips, and hooflike nails on hands and feet, ceratopsids represent a uniform family of dinosaurs that were descended from a single ancestor. Nevertheless, there are two distinct subfamilies – the Chasmosaurinae, and the Centrosaurinae. The horns that are found as fossils in ceratopsians are actually just the bony cores. Just like the horns of cattle, sheep, goats and many other animals, there would have been an outer sheath of horn, which would have been at least 25% longer, and a lot sharper than the bony core. Over the years, there has been a long, sometimes bitter debate over how ceratopsians held their front limbs. Were the arms held directly beneath the shoulder, as modern mammals do, or were the arms held in a sprawling pose? The truth is probably somewhere between the two extremes. Footprints show that the hands were rotated outwards, but that they lined up with the hind feet. This indicates that the elbows were flexed, but were not sprawling.

A chasmosaurine can have a very elongate frill, sometimes reaching the middle of the back. The crests were pierced by large holes, but these would have been covered over by skin. Most have only a short horn on the nose, but the horns over the eyes are long. *Torosaurus* is the largest chasmosaurine, and would have been almost 9 m long, with a weight of 8 tonnes. Like its more common, close relative, *Triceratops*, it was one of the very last dinosaurs. *Triceratops* is found so frequently that many specimens never get collected. Even so, fifteen different species of *Triceratops* have been described over the years, although they probably simply represent the individual and sexual variation of a single species. The easiest way to distinguish the two animals is to look at the frill, because the holes have

Right ~ A family unit of Chasmosaurus endures the discomforts of a violent summer thunderstorm. This dinosaur was one of the more common chasmosaurine ceratopsians in North America 75 million years ago.

Two of the last surviving dinosaurs face off in a modern-looking forest at the end of the Cretaceous. Both Torosaurus and Tyrannosaurus were the largest known forms of their respective families.

been closed up in *Triceratops. Chasmosaurus* lived about 75 million years ago in Alberta, Texas, and presumably everywhere between. In some specimens there are long horns over the eyes, whereas in others the orbital horns are very short. These may be two distinct species, or they may simply be males and females of the same species. All *Chasmosaurus* frills are very long, and are sharply angled at the back. *Anchiceratops* and *Arrhinoceratops* are two large chasmosaurines from Alberta, while *Pentaceratops* is a southern animal found in New Mexico. The name *Pentaceratops* means "five-horn face", and reflects the presence of five horns — one on the nose, one over each eye, and one on each cheek.

Centrosaurine ceratopsids generally have a large horn on the nose, but only small horns over each eye. The frills are shorter, but tend to be ornamented by hooks and spikes. The remains of these dinosaurs are sometimes found in huge bonebeds, showing that they were herding animals. *Centrosaurus* is one of the most common types in Alberta. The horn on the nose can be straight, or it can curve forward or backward. The significance of the curvature is not known. At the back of the frill are two forward-facing spikes. These hooks are also found in a descendant of *Centrosaurus*, although they are barely noticeable because of other, larger spikes on the frill of *Styracosaurus*. One of the most bizarre centrosaurines is *Pachyrhinosaurus*. The bony horn core on the nose has been replaced by a massive boss of bone between the nose and the eyes. It was long assumed that this was the base of a battering ram type of structure. However, the bony boss is similar in size, shape, position and surface texture to the bony thickening in the modern rhinoceros. In the rhino, this is the base of the epidermal horn (made up of aglutinated hair). It is possible that *Pachyrhinosaurus* had a large epidermal horn that sat on the boss. Such a horn would be lighter, stronger and less susceptible to damage. There are other spikes on the frill of *Pachyrhinosaurus*, including a unicorn-like horn rising from the middle of the head at the base of the frill. This dinosaur has been found in bonebeds in Alberta, and males, females, juveniles and babies have been collected. The babies actually resemble the babies of other centrosaurines, and instead of having the huge boss of bone, they have three tiny horns. Such extreme differences related to age suggest that two animals (*Brachylophosaurus, Monoclonius*), long thought to be distinct genera, are just immature centrosaurines.

How Ceratopsids Lived

Like hadrosaurs, ceratopsids had extremely sophisticated dental batteries, made up of many rows of stacked teeth, for chopping and grinding tough plant material. The sharp beak would probably have grasped a low-lying plant or a branch near its base, and a quick twist of the head (possible because of the ball-like joint for the neck) would have broken it off. The powerful jaws and sharp-edged dental batteries would have chopped it into smaller pieces, and the grinding surfaces of the teeth would have crushed it.

Although the horns and frills of ceratopsians may have been used from time to time for defense, they probably evolved more for visual identity, and for fighting with other animals of the same species. Ceratopsian horns and frills demonstrate as much

The frills of ceratopsians are highly variable between species, and provided visual identification that would have helped maintain genetic integrity.

Anchiceratops

Styracosaurus

Pachyrhinosaurus

Chasmosaurus

variety as the horns of modern African antelopes. As with modern horned animals, the horns of ceratopsians were shaped and positioned to interlock when two rival males engaged in combat over females or territory. This diminished the risk of causing serious bodily harm, although there have been reports of holes puncturing the frills of some ceratopsian specimens. Although many of these may be pathologic, some may have been made by rival ceratopsians. The frills may have been used for display. A *Chasmosaurus* would have looked very impressive to a female of his species when he dropped his face to elevate his huge frill. It probably also would have frightened off smaller male rivals.

Ceratopsians, like all animals, were susceptible to disease and injury. Broken ribs are common in *Pachyrhinosaurus*, and it is possible that they rammed each others flanks. One specimen had a huge cyst that had destroyed most of the facial bone beneath the eye. Another specimen had obviously damaged its frill when it was young, for as it grew up the frill became distorted and asymmetrical.

Like hadrosaurs, ceratopsians probably only spent part of the year travelling in herds. *Pachyrhinosaurus* ranged from southern Alberta to the North Slope of Alaska. *Chasmosaurus* went from central Alberta to Texas. As the herds moved from place to place, they were as likely to encounter catastrophes as modern herding animals are. A bonebed in Dinosaur Provincial Park contains the remains of thousands of individuals of *Centrosaurus*. These unfortunate animals apparently were drowned in a river in flood. As individuals, they were probably good swimmers. But en masse, they would obstruct with each other in the water, and if they panicked they would attempt to climb on other individuals, thereby pushing them under water. It sounds fantastic, but mammals, which are supposedly much smarter animals, run into the same problems. For example, over 10,000 caribou drowned in a flooded river in northern Quebec in 1985. The front animals were pushed into the raging waters by the crush of animals behind.

As the sun sets, a hungry pack of dromaeosaurs tries to separate a young ceratopsian from a herd of Styracosaurus. Although faster and more intelligent than the horned dinosaurs, they are unlikely to succeed against such a well-disciplined, well-horned herd.

Right ~ Thescelosaurus flees as a pair of Triceratops males charge and lock horns in a territorial battle that will probably be short but violent.

WHY WERE DINOSAURS SO SUCCESSFUL?

About 350 species of dinosaurs are known at this time, but this represents only a fraction of the number that must have lived. Remember that today there are 8,000 species of birds, 6,000 species of reptiles and amphibians, and 4,000 species of mammals. If we assume that an average species only lasts for about two million years, it is obvious that dinosaurian species changed many times over their 150 million year history. If there were as few as 2,000 species of dinosaurs alive at one time around the world, then 150,000 species of dinosaurs must have existed. This suggests that we presently know less than 0.25 % of the dinosaur species that must have existed. A more conservative way to look at it is to examine the known dinosaurs of a single habitat from a single time period. Dinosaur Provincial Park has between 35 and 50 species of dinosaurs from 75 to 77 million years old. Another 35 species are known from the Nemegt Valley of Mongolia from the same time period. Although this only represents two habitats, they have produced about 20% of the known dinosaur species. If one takes the most conservative figure, and ignores the fact that there were far more than two habitats in the world at any one time, then 70 species, each lasting 2 million years, suggests there must have been at least 5,600 species over the entire history of non avian dinosaurs. No matter how you estimate the total number of species of dinosaurs, it is clear that there are thousands of species remaining to be discovered.

For the most part, dinosaurs were living under favourable climatic conditions that allowed them to spread from one polar region to the other. They were very adaptable animals, and seem to have penetrated every terrestrial ecosystem available to them. At times, populations of dinosaurs would be isolated as the continental land masses pulled apart, or as shallow seas flooded lowlands. New forms would evolve in isolation, and subsequently invade new land masses as continents continued to drift and establish new connections.

Because dinosaurs laid huge nests of eggs every year, there was the potential of adapting rapidly to changing conditions, assuming they were not the catastrophic changes hypothesized as a result of the asteroid hitting the Earth at the end of the Cretaceous.

Dinosaurs clearly had a competitive advantage over other animals in certain types of ecological niches. Although mammals appeared at about the same time as dinosaurs, they remained small, nocturnal animals until dinosaurs disappeared 140 million years later. Dinosaurs dominated the land, and very few species went back to water where they would have been competing with crocodiles, ichthyosaurs, plesiosaurs and mosasaurs. Although the air was exploited successfully by their cousins the pterosaurs, dinosaurs did eventually conquer that frontier through their descendants, the birds. But what were the reasons for the worldwide success of dinosaurs on land?

There are many lines of investigation that have provided insight, but the mystery is unsolved. Anatomical studies show how well dinosaurs became adapted to their ecosystems, developing great size, specialized teeth, horns and claws, improved locomotion, and defensive systems like armour, whips and clubs. Research into dinosaur

The frill of a ceratopsian extended behind the point where the skull attached to the neck. Therefore, when the face rotated downward, the crest was raised. This may have been used to scare away potential predators or rivals, or to attract a mate.

Left ~ One of the most common dinosaurs of the coastal lowlands during Late Cretaceous times, Centrosaurus disturbs a flock of shorebirds by its ponderous movements.

physiology has given some surprising clues on growth rates and metabolism. And behavioural research has shown that dinosaurs were capable of sophisticated behaviour, such as parental care and migration, that is normally attributed to mammals and birds.

Adaptation

The adjustment of an organism to its environment is called adaptation. It can be morphological, physiological, or behavioural. Dinosaurs were remarkably well adapted to their world, and dominated most habitats on land.

Morphological adaptations are shaped by the requirements to find food, shelter and mates in particular environments. Changes occur most readily in the head and limbs, because these are the body parts most involved in feeding and locomotion. There are certain tendencies that are noted in the evolution of any lineage of animals. Animals tend to get larger over time, for example. Dinosaurs did not have a monopoly on large size, and in the past fish, amphibians, turtles, crocodiles, lizards, birds and mammals have all produced gigantic forms. Even humans are showing a tendency to become taller over time. For most animals, being large means that as adults they do not need to worry about predators. Large size is an efficient way to conserve body heat, and it is not necessary to eat as much. Large animals also tend to live longer, and spend less of their time and energies eating and producing young. But as the herbivores get larger, the carnivores are not far behind, and a balance is maintained.

Dinosaurs were the most conspicuous, largest animals throughout the Jurassic and Cretaceous. Forms like *Brachiosaurus* were so large as adults that they would have not worried about predators.

Although there are often many ways to do the same thing, some adaptations are almost universal. Sharp teeth and claws usually evolve in carnivores, while blunt, crushing teeth and hooves are characteristic of herbivores. Animals with similar lifestyles or occupying similar habitats will sometimes look the same, even though they may be completely unrelated. Because of these trends, we can often get clues to the function of certain morphological features in dinosaurs by looking at similar structures in modern animals. The neck of a sauropod, for example, does not look like the neck of any modern aquatic animals, but it does remind of a giraffe's neck. This is one line of evidence to suggest that sauropods browsed high in the trees, and did not feed on aquatic plants.

Physiological Adaptation

Thermoregulation is one aspect of physiology that has been studied for dinosaurs. The idea that dinosaurs might be warm-blooded (endothermic) like mammals and birds was initially proposed more than forty years ago by a Canadian palaeontologist, Dr. Loris Russell. It was not until *Deinonychus* was discovered and described by John Ostrom that the idea was taken seriously, however. *Deinonychus*, an Early Cretaceous relative of *Velociraptor*, was small, intelligent, and probably very nasty. It was also very birdlike, and reopened the question of whether or not birds were descended from dinosaurs. The idea that such a fast, energetic looking animal might be warm-blooded was championed by Robert T. Bakker, who started to look at many lines of evidence,

Right ~ Lying peacefully on a bed of moss and ferns beside a stream, a gorged tyrannosaur digests its last meal. Larger and more robust than Albertosaurus, but smaller than Tyrannosaurus, Daspletosaurus may have specialized in killing ceratopsians.

including the microscopic structure of their bones, the ratio of predatory dinosaurs to prey, growth rates, locomotory dynamics, and colonization of polar regions. Improved and entirely erect limbs justify the hypothesis that dinosaurs were active animals that needed high energy output. As scientists started to look at dinosaur footprints in the late 1970s, they could see that dinosaurs walked upright with their tails held high above the ground. The maximum running speed of an animal generally depends on the relative lengths and proportions of its legs. However, only a warm-blooded animal can produce enough energy to run fast for a long time. Dinosaurs had long and fully erect limbs. A mathematical formula was developed to determine how fast an animal was moving when it made a trackway, so dinosaur trackways can be used to estimate the speeds that dinosaurs were actually running. The tracks were almost invariably made in mud, otherwise they would not have been preserved, and it is doubtful that dinosaurs would have been running at their fastest in such slippery conditions. Nevertheless, trackways have been found in Texas that show dinosaurs could run in excess of 25 km/hour. The

Many animals have shown a tendency to get larger over long periods of time. One of the largest mammals was *Indricotherium*, a giant rhinoceros from central Asia that was as large as most sauropods.

The protoceratopsian Montanoceratops was a relatively primitive dinosaur that could not compete with its larger, more specialized ceratopsid relatives. It therefore lived in habitats avoided by most other dinosaurs, and in the highlands of North America it no doubt had to endure the occasional snowfall.

carnivorous dinosaurs were almost invariably moving faster than the herbivores. These figures confirm that dinosaurs were active animals, but do not necessarily prove that they were warm-blooded.

In fossilization, the microscopic spaces inside bones are infilled by minerals, but the original bone remains largely unchanged. Many dinosaur bones have been preserved in such good state that they can be cut by a microtome equally well as the bones of living animals. This makes it possible to study the microscopic structure (histology) of their bones. One indicator of cold blooded (ectothermic) physiology is the presence of growth rings in the bone, similar to the rings in tree trunks and branches. Growth rings indicate changes in growth rates throughout the year. Growth will slow down when the climate is cold (winter) or dry, and will speed up when it is warm (summer) or wet. Differences in the speed of growth produces differences in the density of the bone, thereby producing a seasonally controlled alternation of rings of relatively high and low density. Growth rings are found in some of the contemporaries of the dinosaurs, such as crocodiles and champsosaurs. But this type of growth ring is never found in a dinosaur. Histological work by Jack Horner and his colleagues also confirms that dinosaurs had very high growth rates, again like mammals and birds rather than reptiles.

Other evidence can be obtained from the histological study of bones. Armand de Ricqles (University of Paris) and others have ascertained that dinosaur bones are structurally closer to the bones of mammals and birds than they are to any living reptiles. In warm-blooded animals, the bone is rebuilt internally as the animal grows, and it has many internal passages for blood vessels. Dinosaurs have this type of microscopic bone structure, not the type that is found in reptiles.

Histological studies of bone have also shown that dinosaurs grew at tremendous rates. This is not too surprising because most baby dinosaurs were tiny compared to their parents. A baby *Mamenchisaurus*, if hatched from an egg, would have been up to 2 m in length, and the adults could become 25 m long. With such a huge difference between babies and adults, there would be a selective advantage for fast growth. The rates dinosaurs grew are similar to those of warm-blooded mammals and birds. Experts suspect dinosaurs could only maintain such growth rates if they had a constantly high body temperatures like birds and mammals. But does it mean that they were warm-blooded?

Predator/prey ratios provide yet another line of evidence of physiology. In any ecosystem, the number of carnivores is limited by the available food: the population of herbivores. If the number of meat-eaters increases, then they need to kill more herbivores so they can eat. If the balance is upset too much, then food availability for the carnivores decreases, and they die back. Although a balance is always maintained between predators and prey, the balanced ratio is significantly different between cold-blooded and warm-blooded predators. Because endothermic animals require more energy, warm-blooded carnivorous animals need more food, and

Meat-eating animals generally have sharp recurved claws for killing other animals, holding struggling prey, and tearing up a carcass. The claws of plant-eating dinosaurs, because of a need to support relatively heavier bodies, have become broad, flattened and hoof-like.

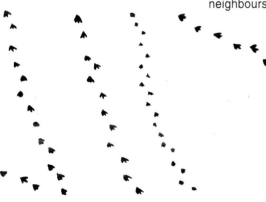

Dinosaur footprints in trackways provide information on what dinosaurs were doing when they were still alive. The four animals that made these tracks appear to have been walking side by side because when one individual moved too far to one side, it affected the paths of its neighbours.

A giant bonebed in Dinosaur Provincial Park in Alberta documents a mass death where thousands of individuals in a herd of *Centrosaurus* may have drowned. After the animals died, they were scavenged. The remaining muscles and ligaments of the torn-apart carcasses rotted away, and when the ancient river went into flood phase, the bones were mixed up in the currents, and then buried by sand and mud.

kill more prey than cold-blooded carnivores. For instance, a wild dog devours its own weight in meat each week. On the other hand, it takes a broad-backed varanid lizard, which is cold-blooded, about two months to eat its own weight in meat. It follows that the warm-blooded population must contain a much smaller ratio of carnivores than herbivorous species, otherwise the prey would be quickly depleted. Cold-blooded carnivores can make up between 10 and 50 % of a population, whereas warm-blooded carnivores are usually only 5 %. Because Dinosaur Provincial Park in Alberta had produced so many dinosaur skeletons over the years, it was a good place to check the predator/prey ratio. The predators only made up about 5% of the population, suggesting that they may have been warm blooded.

It is well known that small warm-blooded animals need hair, feathers or some form of insulation to maintain their high body temperatures. As animals increase in size, the surface area does not increase as fast as the volume or mass. Consequently,

Above ~ Two large male Triceratops are not hesitant about chasing away a young inexperienced tyrannosaur that happens to get too close to the main herd.

big animals have much smaller surface areas (skin) compared to their weight than small animals. Because of this, the larger an animal is, the less rapidly it loses its body heat. Big dinosaurs, therefore, could control their temperature more easily than small ones. Small dinosaurs would have had a problem maintaining their body temperatures if they were warm-blooded, unless they had some form of insulation. Although no dinosaur fossils have been found with feathers, it is assumed that feathers developed in dinosaurs for insulation and were only adapted for flight later in birds. Many dinosaurs had developed a secondary palate to enable them to breathe when eating. As warm-blooded animals must breathe all the time, this characteristic also suggests dinosaurs were physiologically closer to birds and mammals.

Further proof is found in the vertebrae of most saurischian dinosaurs. The vertebrae were hollow at the front of the body, and in life would have been filled by air sacs that were connected to the lungs. In birds, these sacs permit effective and efficient exchange of gases in the lungs.

Edmontosaurus herds ranged along the coastal lowlands between Alberta and Alaska 70 million years ago. This is one dinosaur that seems to have preferred wet, marshy habitats.

It has not been completely resolved whether or not dinosaurs were warm-blooded or cold-blooded animals. Because of the large body size of most dinosaurs, they would have been functionally warm-blooded (homeothermic) anyway, and would not have changed their core temperature very rapidly. The smaller dinosaurs would have had difficulty in controlling their body temperatures unless they were endotherms. But no argument has been completely convincing, and the majority of palaeontologists believe that only some dinosaurs, specifically the small theropods, were warm-blooded. Part of the problem may be that we rely too much on comparisons with modern animals, and perhaps dinosaurs were doing something quite different from either cold-blooded reptiles or warm-blooded mammals and birds. In recent years, some have suggested that dinosaurs may have been endothermic when they were born, but ectothermic as their body size became large. In that way, they could take advantage of both systems. Although it sounds fantastic, even modern animals can change their thermal metabolism. Some birds are ectothermic when they are born, for example, but become endothermic as they grow up.

Behavioural Adaptations

Behavioural adaptations cannot be seen in the fossil record. However, it can be shown using evidence from footprints and bonebeds that some herbivorous dinosaurs gathered into enormous herds, while some carnivores formed packs, presumably for group hunting. There are numerous advantages to both kinds of behaviour. For the plant-eaters the main advantage was probably protection, whereas a pack of carnivores would be able to bring down and kill larger prey than a single predator could. Many dinosaurs appear to have been gregarious. *Iguanodon* specimens from Belgium, *Plateosaurus* from Germany, *Maiasaura* from Montana, and *Edmontosaurus* from Alaska are just a few examples of herding dinosaurs.

The duck-like bill of a hadrosaur can be seen easily from the top. The mouth is broad and flat at the front, perfect for gathering up large amounts of vegetation.

In 1978, a concentration of ceratopsian bones was found in Dinosaur Provincial Park in Alberta. The site was excavated over a period of more than a decade, and produced the remains of more than 80 individuals of *Centrosaurus*. Because only

147

Dinosaur eggs were first discovered in the Gobi Desert by the American Museum of Natural History expedition in 1922. Elongate eggs are common at sites where protoceratopsians are common, and it is assumed that the eggs were laid by *Protoceratops*.

a small portion of the bonebed was excavated, the estimated number of dead animals was in the hundreds. Recently it was discovered that the bonebed actually follows an ancient stream channel and is at least 8 kilometres long, and the estimated number of dead *Centrosaurus* must be many thousands. Palaeontological and geological research on the site suggests that a herd of *Centrosaurus* tried to cross a river in flood, and that many drowned as the animals at the front of the herd were pushed into the raging waters by those behind. The carcasses came to rest along the course of the river, where they were left on the banks and sandbars as the waters receded. Carnivores moved in and stripped the bones of their flesh, and the bones were eventually buried when the river went into a subsequent flood phase.

The gregarious behaviour of some dinosaurs needs to be explained. After all, thousands of multi-tonne animals could not have stayed in one area for long because they would destroy all of the plants. One of the most common reasons modern animals gather into large herds is to migrate. Migration allows animals to exploit resources that may only be abundant for part of the year. It also provides opportunities to colonize and invade new regions. Like today, some regions during Mesozoic times would have been susceptible to periodic or seasonal droughts. This seems to have been the case in some parts of North America during Late Jurassic times. To cope with the seasonal droughts, sauropods and other dinosaurs would collect into herds and move to areas where the food was more plentiful.

In 1985, the Universities of California and Alaska opened up an excavation on the North Slope of Alaska within the Arctic Circle. Dinosaur bones had been discovered there in 1967, although they were not recognized as such for more than fifteen years. Arctic dinosaur remains have also been found in the Yukon and northwest territories of Canada, and in Siberia. On the other side of the globe, Australia and Antarctica were within the Antarctic Circle during Early Cretaceous times, and both continents have produced dinosaurs. Although the polar regions were much warmer in Mesozoic times than today (we actually are living in a relatively cold period in the Earth's history), they were still dark during the winter months. At that time, the plants would become dormant, and there would not be enough food available for large herbivorous dinosaurs. Although smaller animals may have hibernated, the long legged hadrosaurs, ceratopsians and tyrannosaurs had the option of moving to latitudes where food was more plentiful during winter. When summer came, they would be back in the polar regions, however, because the hours of daily sunshine stimulated high plant growth. These long migrations were safer for herbivores if they moved en masse, so they would collect into great herds. Sometimes these herds would encounter natural disasters, and hundreds, or even thousands of animals would die. The *Centrosaurus* bonebed described above is one example. But other bonebeds dominated by single species of animals have been found in Alberta, Alaska, Montana, and Texas and provide further evidence that such catastrophes did occur.

Migrations can also occur between regions, and do not have to be cyclic. As the continents shifted positions, connections were made and broken between land masses. And when these land bridges formed, dinosaurs and other animals would move across them to colonize new regions. This can be confirmed by the fact that Asia and western North America had very similar dinosaur faunas during the Late Cretaceous. Tyrannosaurs, dromaeosaurids, troodontids, ornithomimids, hadrosaurs, protoceratopsids and ankylosaurids are some of the animals that were moving between the continents. Europe had connections to eastern North America, and the same Early Jurassic species are found in Nova Scotia, Greenland and Germany.

Another aspect of behaviour is parental care. Because baby dinosaurs were so small next to their parents, they were probably very vulnerable to the attacks of carnivores. Parental protection was one way to reduce the hazards of early life.

Jack Horner, the dinosaur palae-ontologist at the Museum of the Rockies (Bozeman), has been collecting dinosaur eggs, embryos and babies from the Upper Cretaceous rocks of Montana for more than fifteen years.

Eggs and Nests

Ever since dinosaurs were discovered, it was assumed that they laid eggs like modern reptiles. Few thought about recovering fossilized eggs, because eggs are very fragile and easily destroyed. In 1869, Philippe Matheron published a paper in Marseilles in which he reported the discovery of fossil reptile bones in the sediments near Fuveau in southern France. He described the remains of one dinosaur as *Hypselosaurus priscus*, a sauropod. Egg shell fragments were discovered in abundance in the same Upper Cretaceous rocks, and Matheron believed they were either from the sauropod, or from a large, unknown bird. These egg shells were studied by other experts over the years, but none could determine for sure if they were from dinosaur eggs. The question remained open until 1928, when Victor van Straelen, director of the museum in Brussels, had a chance to compare the microstructure of the European egg shell to that of unquestionable dinosaur eggs that had been discovered in the Gobi Desert. He was convinced that the shell fragments were from giant eggs laid by *Hypselosaurus*.

Hadrosaur eggs were almost perfectly round, and were encased in hard shells like bird eggs. Although hadrosaurs could grow to more than 10 m in length, the diameter of a hadrosaur egg is less than 25 cm.

149

One line of evidence that suggests dinosaurs were warm-blooded is the microscopic structure of the bones. The bones are well supplied with blood vessels, and show the evidence of destruction and redeposition that is characteristic of rapidly-growing, warm-blooded animals. Rapid growth is unquestionable.

Soon afterwards, in 1930, a French farmer digging in his vineyard found a complete fossil egg. Many more discoveries were to follow in southern France and northern Spain, and hundreds of complete eggs have been collected from the region, as well as millions of fragments.

As was already said on page 14, the Third Central Asiatic Expedition of the American Museum of Natural History, which set out in 1922 to discover if Asia was the birthplace of man, was one of the last large scale dinosaur-hunting expeditions, until money became available again in the 1970s.

Above ~ The good mother reptile, Maiasaura, buries her nest of newly laid eggs with sand and wet vegetation. As the plants decompose, they produce heat to incubate the eggs, something that the mother is too heavy to do herself.

Dinosaur eggs found in the 1920s made the expeditions famous worldwide. Some of the dinosaur eggs were elongate, with a length of 25 cm, and a 20 cm circumference. Small white inclusions were interpreted as the remains of embryonic bones. We now know that they are mineral inclusions, not bones, but at that time they created quite a sensation. The egg shell preserved its microstructure, and was hard like the shell of birds, rather than being leathery as in turtles and crocodiles.

Members of the expedition found more nests with smaller, smooth-shelled eggs. Although they did not recognize that these were laid by different dinosaurs, they recovered at least four types of eggs from the Flaming Cliffs. Associated with the eggs were the remains of *Protoceratops* skeletons, representing newly-hatched babies to large adults. It was assumed that most of the eggs had been laid by this common dinosaur. However, unless embryos are found within the eggs, it is difficult to prove that any type of egg was laid by a particular dinosaur. The expedition returned to the Flaming Cliffs in 1925, and in the meantime had discovered Late Cretaceous dinosaur eggs at another site in China. By then, it had been recognized that the nests were probably scooped out of the sand by the mother, who then laid the eggs in a spiral up to three layers thick. The region was semi-arid during the Cretaceous, and when sand storms raged, they would sometimes bury the eggs so deeply that the embryos inside would suffocate and die. As the contents rotted, the pressure of the accumulated sand would crack the eggs, and fine sand would filter inside.

We are not sure how dinosaurs mated, but imagine it was the same as their modern relatives, crocodiles and birds. Broken bones at the base of the tail in some specimens suggest that mating was sometimes hazardous for the females.

Fragments of dinosaur egg shell had been recovered from the Cretaceous deposits of Alberta, Montana, and Utah for many years. It was not until the end of the 1970s that significant egg discoveries were made. In 1978 the well-known dinosaur hunter, Jack Horner, and his colleague Bob Makela went into a store that sold fossils, and found the tiny bones of what they thought were newly hatched dinosaurs. The store owner led Horner and Makela to the site where the bones were discovered. Subsequent excavation revealed a nest with fifteen baby hadrosaurs, each about 60 cm long, and an enormous quantity of broken egg shells. The teeth of the babies were worn, but the ends of the bones were poorly formed. These two facts suggest that the animals were eating, but that they were incapable of walking very far. Because the babies were thought to have been several months old, it was evident that food was being brought to them by one or both parents. The bones of adults were found nearby, and the new type of hadrosaur was named *Maiasaura*, which means the "good mother reptile". Since the first discovery was made, many nests, embryos and hatchlings have been found in the same region west of Choteau, Montana. Nests found concentrated in one area were separated by a distance (7 m) equivalent to the length of an adult *Maiasaura*. 14 nests, 42 eggs and 31 young were collected. *Maiasaura* nested in colonies, much as gulls and many other species of modern birds do, and the nests were separated by enough room to allow the adults to walk between them safely.

Each *Maiasaura* nest contains about two dozen eggs, each about 20 cm long. The nests were one to two metres across, and a half metre deep. There were plant remains associated with the eggs, and it is possible that the parents covered the nests with vegetation. As the vegetation rotted, it would produce heat and incubate the eggs. Obviously a four tonne mother could not have sat on her eggs. Once the eggs hatched, food (possibly regurgitated berries) was brought to the young until they were large enough to follow the adults. Once they were large enough, they would have been able to join the herds. One of these herds suffered some kind of a natural catastrophe, possibly an ash fall from a volcano. The resulting bonebed contains the remains of more than 10,000 hadrosaurs.

Colonial nesting improves the chances of survival of young animals, even though the young in nests at the periphery of the colony were probably easy prey for carnivores. Not surprisingly, teeth of *Albertosaurus*, *Troodon* and *Saurornitholestes* are often found in the nests mixed with baby bones. However, the vast majority of babies would have survived.

Many nests have been found in western Montana of the hypsilophodont *Orodromeus makeli*. These animals were breeding and reproducing in the same area as *Maiasaura*. In 1987, another major nesting site was found in Devil's Coulee, southern Alberta. At this locality, the eggs had been laid by the hadrosaur *Hypacrosaurus*. Every stage from embryos to adults has been recovered, and this is the best growth series known for a hadrosaur.

Dinosaur Brains

The size of a dinosaur brain can be determined by looking at the cavity within the braincase, those bones of the skull that surround the brain. Most dinosaurs had relatively small brains, although they are not as small as most people think. A sauropod brain, for example, is certainly minute if you compare it to the size of its body. However, there is a tendency for the ratio between brain weight and body weight to decrease as any animal gets bigger. A bigger brain is not necessarily needed in a bigger body because it is still controlling the same number of muscles and joints. In a sauropod, even its relatively small brain was more than adequate to meet the demands made on it, and we know that sauropods were animals with complex behaviour.

All dinosaurs did not have small brains either. *Troodon* had a brain that was six times the size of the brain of a crocodile with its body size. Dromaeosaurids and ornithomimids also had relatively large brains that fall within the lower end of the scale for modern mammals and birds.

The relationship between brain size and intelligence is poorly understood in modern animals, and it is even harder to make such comparisons in animals that are no longer around. Nevertheless, it is generally assumed that there is a direct relationship between brain size and intelligence.

The cavity inside the braincase is not a smooth walled hole in the head. It is contoured to match the outer surface of the brain itself, and it is pierced by holes for the nerves and blood vessels. Study of casts made of the hollow interior of the braincase can therefore give palaeontologists a lot more information than just the size. The relative

In North America, herds of dinosaurs migrated north and south between the western mountains and the epicontinental seas that covered most of the interior of the continent.

Right ~ As the sun sets, a Prosaurolophus stretches out in the dense undergrowth of a coastal forest. Like other flat-headed hadrosaurs, it seems to have preferred wetter, more heavily vegetated environments than the crested hadrosaurs.

sizes of the different lobes of the brain can indicate which senses were developed, and whether an animal had good motor control.

The Environment

Natural environments are the sum of all the conditions enabling an organism to live in a certain place, and to develop and multiply. We know that dinosaurs probably lived in all types of terrestrial environments that were available to them. Their remains are most frequently found from environments that were associated with rivers, streams, lakes and ponds. However, the higher frequency is related to better opportunities of animal remains to become fossilized in these kinds of environments.

Animals only occupy environments where food is available to them. Food does not necessarily need to be abundant, as long as competition for limited resources is not problematic. Consequently, harsher environments have much lower species diversity. Compare, for example, the lush coastal lowlands that existed in Dinosaur Provincial Park with the semi-arid Cretaceous environments of central Asia. In Dinosaur Provincial Park, more than 35 species of dinosaurs have been identified, whereas a central Asian site like the Flaming Cliffs has yielded only eight species, even though both localities have produced hundreds of skeletons. Dinosaur remains have also been discovered in the polar regions, in intermontane basins, and on islands.

The discovery of dinosaur skeletons in rocks of certain types usually provides good evidence of where those dinosaurs were living. Most of the dinosaur skeletons recovered in Dinosaur Provincial Park are probably from animals that lived in that region 75 million years ago. Carcasses and bones can be carried great distances from where the animals died, however, so one needs to analyse the evidence carefully. Dinosaur bones are sometimes found in marine sediments. The carcass of a dead dinosaur, bloated by gases in the body cavity, could have been carried down a river system and then floated out to sea. The discovery of the skeleton in marine sediments is therefore not an indication that the dinosaur lived in the sea.

Bones can also be buried and reworked many times by water action. Dinosaur bones have been found in Palaeocene beds in Montana and New Mexico, in Eocene rocks in Saskatchewan, and in Pleistocene deposits in Alberta. The dinosaurs that provided the bones all died before the end of the Cretaceous, but their bones kept getting washed out of the older rocks to be reburied in younger sediments. These represent relatively uncommon occurrences, and if they were more common or of a different nature, then the conclusions reached might be very different. The fact that *Corythosaurus* skeletons are very common in Dinosaur Provincial Park is a good indication that *Corythosaurus* actually lived there. Only one *Parasaurolophus* has been found in the Park, so it cannot be determined with certainty whether this animal lived there, or if its body was carried in from farther upstream. The discovery of an articulated skeleton of a dinosaur above the Cretaceous-Tertiary boundary would cause a sensation, because whole skeletons are unlikely to be reworked, and such a discovery would be strong evidence that all dinosaurs did not die out at the end of the Cretaceous.

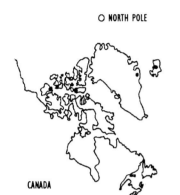

O NORTH POLE

CANADA

This polar projection of Earth shows sites where dinosaurs have been collected inside the Arctic Circle. Some of these dinosaurs were fossilized when the continents were farther south, but most spent at least part of each year in the Arctic.

The discovery of nests of dinosaur eggs in the ancient deserts of central Asia is convincing proof that some dinosaurs could live under very harsh conditions. This nest was excavated by the American Museum of Natural History expedition in 1923.

Right ~ A pair of Eoceratops are seeking a suitable place to bed down as the moon, enlarged and reddened by the thick atmosphere, rises above the horizon.

A dinosaur brain is usually studied by making a rubber cast of the brain cavity inside the skull. In addition to providing information on the shape, size and composition of the brain, the cranial nerves can also be studied.

Eggs and nests of dinosaurs cannot be moved any great distance without being destroyed. The discovery of a nest of dinosaur eggs therefore means that dinosaurs were at one time living at that site. The large numbers of nests found in the 80 million year old desert rocks of central Asia indicate that dinosaurs were living in those ancient deserts.

Footprints clearly show where dinosaurs walked. They cannot be transported, and are easily destroyed by river and stream action. Although very few dinosaur bones are found in Korea, there are thousands of dinosaur footprints that clearly show many types of dinosaurs once lived there. Theropod footprints found in the ancient floors of stream channels show that the meat-eating dinosaurs were not afraid of going into the water, and would chase prey there.

Fossilized excrement, coprolites, are quite common at some sites. The contents of coprolites have been analyzed in some cases, and give clues about which animals and plants lived with the coprolite maker. Teeth and fish scales are more likely to survive the digestive system than plant remains are. Consequently, coprolites usually give the best information on carnivores.

The context in which fossils are found often provides good information on the environment in which the dinosaur was living. A *Pentaceratops* skeleton discovered in New Mexico was associated with leaves and branches of the plants living beside the stream channel in which the carcass was buried. Sedimentologists can look at the structures and composition of the rock, and determine how wide the stream was, and how fast the current might have been. Other associated fossils can give further information on the environment. Frogs and piscidiid clams, for example, live in the quiet waters of ponds and marshes, while salamanders can be found on land or in mountain streams.

Raising its head above the morning mist, Gryposaurus relies on its good eyesight and sense of hearing to warn it of any approaching carnivores.

Right ~ Startled by the sight of an approaching tornado, a Saurolophus moves with amazing speed and agility for an animal of its size.

The Great Extinction

At the end of the Cretaceous, 65 million years ago, all dinosaurs except birds seem to have died out. The fossil record is not complete, and we do not know for sure they disappeared everywhere on the Earth at the same time. Some dinosaur fossils have been found in the rocks above the Cretaceous-Tertiary boundary, but as discussed before, they are probably reworked from older sediments.

Dinosaurs were not the only animals that disappeared at the end of the Cretaceous. Many of the other great reptiles, including mosasaurs, plesiosaurs and pterosaurs disappeared at the same time. Major lineages of invertebrates also perished. Conspicuous is the extinction of ammonites, the shelled, squid-like animals that dominated the Mesozoic seas. The disappearance of many types of micro-organisms suggests that the whole marine ecosystem had collapsed.

Extinction is normal for any species, most of which only last for about 2 million years. But although dinosaur species evolved and died out throughout the Mesozoic, there can be no doubt that the extinction event at the end of the Cretaceous was devastating.

Some palaeontologists believe that the extinction was catastrophic, while others believe that it was gradual, lasting millions of years. There is strong evidence in favour of both theories, and it may be that the truth is a combination of both.

For a long time, the belief prevailed that dinosaur extinction was the result of climatic change. At the end of the Cretaceous, there were major changes as inland seas regressed and mountains were pushed up on many of the continents. As the seas withdrew from Asia and North America, their moderating effect on the climates would have ceased, and seasonal changes would have become more extreme. More extreme climates would have reduced the amount of dinosaur diversity.

In support of the gradualist theory of extinction, evidence from Alberta, Montana and Wyoming suggests that dinosaur diversity started to decline about 7 million years before the end of the Cretaceous. 76 million years ago, thirty families of dinosaurs are known. But by the end of the Cretaceous, only twelve families remain.

Some believe gradual climatic change could have eventually driven dinosaurs to extinction. However, dinosaurs could tolerate extreme climates, especially those that lived in the polar regions. Crocodiles, lizards, snakes and many other animals were unable to tolerate Cretaceous Arctic conditions, yet they survived the Cretaceous. A study on the turtles above and below the Cretaceous-Tertiary boundary in Montana shows that between fifteen and seventeen of the nineteen Cretaceous types survived the extinction event. Gradual climatic change does not seem to be a supportable cause for the massive extinctions.

The leading hypothesis for catastrophic destruction of dinosaurs postulates that an asteroid hit the Earth 65 million years ago. L. W. Alvarez and his colleagues in 1980

Dinosaur teeth have been found in rocks younger than the end of the Cretaceous, suggesting that some dinosaurs may not have died out at the time of the Great Extinction event. However, fossils eroded from older rocks can be reburied in younger rocks, so scientists need to be cautious.

Left ~ An alert Arrhinoceratops is aroused from its sleep by a sound in the forest, and peers intensely into the cold, clear night air. Well developed senses of sight, hearing and smell generally gave ceratopsians adequate warning of theropod movements.

THE DINOSAUROID

What would have happened if dinosaurs had not died out? This question tempted palaeontologist Dale Russell and artist A. R. Seguin of the Canadian Museum of Nature to conduct a thought experiment in 1982. Focussing on *Stenonychosaurus,* now known as *Troodon*, they speculated that the brain would have continued to grow in relative size, which would have forced corresponding changes in the skull. The large, heavy head would have required the support of a vertical backbone. The large eyes would have faced forward, but the ears would have retained the three fingers to manipulate food. The resulting animal, as conceived in a sculpture, looks rather humanoid. At 140 cm of height, it would only weigh 42 kg. Because *Troodon* did become extinct, there is no way to know what potential descendants might have become. The Dinosauroid is fantasy, not science. But its human-like image forcefully made the point that dinosaurs were evolving into more sophisticated animals when their future was terminated by extinction.

ascertained that a thin layer of sediments at the Cretaceous-Tertiary boundary contained relatively higher quantities of iridium and other metals of the platinum group. This anomaly is found associated with boundary sediments, both marine and terrestrial, around the world. Because iridium normally is only found in high quantities in asteroids, meteorites and other extra-terrestrial sources, it seemed possible that an asteroid, perhaps 10 km across, may have collided with the Earth. The hypothesis has inspired numerous geochemical, lithological and palaeontological studies that have produced an impressive body of evidence supporting the impact theory. The possible impact site has even been found in the Yucatan Peninsula of Mexico.

The dust cloud resulting from an asteroid impact would have shielded the surface of the planet from sunlight for perhaps several months. Without sunlight, the plants died off. Without plants, the plant-eating dinosaurs perished. And without them the carnivores were doomed. Similar chain reactions would have occurred in the oceans. The plants themselves would have mostly recovered (seeds can usually survive extreme conditions), and the smaller animals could have survived the difficult period by eating seeds and detritus.

It seems like an elegant, simple theory to explain the great extinction event. But the impact theory cannot explain why fresh water communities of animals were not affected, whereas marine environments were.

Not everyone is convinced that an asteroid hit the Earth. Iridium can also be brought up from deep within the Earth by volcanoes. If this were the source of the iridium, it could explain other iridium-enhanced layers well below and above the Cretaceous-Tertiary boundary. There was a lot of volcanic activity at the end of the Cretaceous, testified to by enormous basalt effusions forming the Deccan tableland, which covers some 600,000 square kilometres in western India. They are one of the largest volcanic effusions known for this planet over the last 200 million years. Observation of the effects of recent eruptions suggests that enormous quantities ($1,300 \times 10^6$ tonnes) of sulphur dioxide would have been ejected into the atmosphere. The result would have been acid rain around the world. As it fell in the oceans, together with great quantities of carbon dioxide, it would have reduced the alkalinity of the marine waters from pH = 8.2 to a pH of less than 7.4. Modern eruptions, if they are large enough, can also cause climatic cooling, and the eruptions that caused the Deccan traps must have had major effects on the climate. It is estimated that they would have cooled the atmosphere by 3.1°C averaged over the year. Hydrochloric acid thrown into the stratosphere would also have caused a substantial reduction of the ozone layer. This would have resulted in a considerable increase in the intensity of ultraviolet radiation, which is harmful to life.

These changes were extremely disruptive, and explain the extinction of warm-climate organisms and the extinction of sea plankton. Plankton with calcareous shells (foraminiferans and coccolithians) would have been affected the most because of the reduction of alkalinity near the surfaces of the oceans. Only non-specialized foraminiferans persevered. The reduced alkalinity did not affect every type of organism. The Dinoflagellata of the Flagellata were the least affected, but we know that some of their recent descendants can tolerate pH values of less than 5.0.

Right ~ Parasaurolophus had the most fantastic crest known in a lambeosaurine hadrosaur. The nasal passages went from the nostrils to the end of the crest, then doubled back within the crest to open into the throat.

A unique combination of the volcanic and impact theories relates to the Deccan Traps of India. Perhaps all the volcanism in that region was triggered by an impact. Computations suggest that a ten kilometre wide asteroid would penetrate the Earth's crust to a depth of 20 to 40 km, providing a channel through which the magma could rise.

The deliberations on the extinction event at the end of the Cretaceous must take into account many facts. First, dinosaurs were not the only animals affected, and extinctions were occurring simultaneously in the seas. Second, many plants and animals show little or no change across the boundary. In western North America there is a short term change at the boundary which suggests plant communities were disrupted, but recovered. There is a change of character of sedimentation from the prevailing carbonate type of the Late Cretaceous to a siliciclastic regime after the boundary. Stable isotopes show a heavy fluctuation in the $^{13}C/^{12}C$ and $^{18}0/^{15}0$ ratios above and below the Cretaceous-Tertiary boundary.

At present, no extinction theories are universally accepted by palaeontologists, geologists and other experts working on extinction problems. The evidence to suggest an asteroid hit the Earth 65 million years ago is strong. But so is the evidence supporting gradual reduction of dinosaur diversity over the last several million years of the Cretaceous. A lot more evidence is needed to determine whether these effects were universal. Did dinosaurs die out at the same time everywhere in the world? We do not know. Did they die out gradually everywhere as they seem to have been doing in western North America? We do not know. Dinosaur extinction remains one of the great mysteries of the Earth, and it will probably puzzle scientists for many generations to come.

DINOSAUR EXTINCTION THEORIES

Hundreds of theories have been proposed to explain dinosaur extinction. No theory is universally accepted, and dinosaur extinction remains one of the Earth's great mysteries.

Extinction might have been caused by:

Birth of babies of only one sex

Collision with asteroid or comet

Competition with mammals

Cooling climates

Disease

Ecological collapse

Egg-shell thinning

Infertility

Oxygen imbalance in atmosphere

Poisons in new species of plants

Radiation from a supernova of neighbouring star

Volcanism

Warming climates

DINOSAUR EXPEDITIONS AROUND THE WORLD

In 1886, 44 years after the discovery of dinosaur bones in England, the remains of these giant reptiles were found in Africa. These included specimens described by British scientists as *Massospondylus* and *Euskelosaurus*. Around 1900, numerous new discoveries were made by the Scottish doctor Robert Broom, who spent most of his professional career in South Africa. He is most famous for collecting numerous skeletons of mammal-like reptiles, but found dinosaur skeletons too. More recently (since c. 1960), A. W. Crompton and Alan Charig (British Museum of Natural History) made discoveries in Lesotho, while French scientists (Albert de Laparrent and Philippe Taquet) worked in the Sahara, in the Atlas Mountains of Morocco, on Madagascar, and elsewhere. Other dinosaur sites are known in Algeria, Egypt, Kenya, Malawi, Niger, Tunisia and Zimbabwe.

The most famous African finds, however, came from the Tendaguru locality of Tanzania. An expedition headed by Werner Janensch found enormous quantities of Jurassic dinosaurs between 1909 and 1912. *Brachiosaurus*, *Dicraeosaurus*, *Kentrosaurus* and other specimens on display in Berlin demonstrate how successful this expedition was. British expeditions went to Tendaguru in later years, and it was here that Louis Leakey, a name associated with some of the most spectacular finds of early man, learned how to collect fossils.

In 1993, an international expedition led by Dr. Paul Sereno (University of Chicago) collected several skeletons of a new type of large sauropod from the deserts of Niger.

The first finds of South American dinosaurs were made in 1882 by the well-known brothers Ameghino. Carlos Ameghino collected specimens, and worked chiefly in the field, while Florentino studied and described the discoveries. As early as 1920, dinosaur bones from different regions of Argentina were deposited in the museum in La Plata. They were mostly sauropods and dinosaurs that inhabited the regions full of rivers, bogs and lakes. The German explorer, Friedrich von Huene, worked in South America, where he found the remains of prosauropods in the Triassic sediments of southern Brazil. In these regions, *Staurikosaurus* was found, and is still one of the oldest and most primitive dinosaurs known. More recently, dinosaur collecting programs have been operated by Argentine museums, mostly under the direction of José Bonaparte. Armour-plated sauropods, horned theropods, peculiar small theropods, hadrosaurs, and many other fascinating specimens have been recovered. Two of the most exciting finds are presently the earliest records. *Herrerasaurus* and *Eoraptor* are two early theropods that are very close to the origin of both ornithischians and saurischians. These and other finds have made Argentina one of the hot spots for dinosaur collecting.

Friedrich von Huene was a famous palaeontologist and explorer from Germany. He was one of the first to collect dinosaurs in South America, where he walked distances that are inconceivable to modern travellers.

When people think of dinosaurs, they certainly do not think of Antarctica. Yet in the past this continent was ice-free, and was covered by great forests. At times it was connected to India and Australia, and formed a bridge between the two regions. In 1987, the palaeontologist Zulmo Gasparini acquainted the Tenth Congress of Brazilian Palaeontologists with the first find of dinosaurs from Antarctica. A specimen had been discovered at the northern end of James Ross Island in the sandstones of an ancient shallow, marine bay. The specimen appears to have been flushed into the bay by an ancient river. The 80 million year old Cretaceous rocks had yielded the remains of an ankylosaur, which are even rarer in the southern hemisphere than they are in the north. A specimen from Patagonia identified as an ankylosaur by von Huene had long been considered as an incorrect identification. But this and other specimens from Australia and India seem more plausible since the Antarctic discovery. It provides the bridge necessary for understanding the distribution of not only dinosaurs, but many other animals and plants on the southern continents. It provides yet more evidence for continental drift.

Since the initial discovery, several more dinosaurs have been discovered on Antarctica. The British Museum of Natural History recovered a well preserved hypsilophodont. An American group made a more spectacular discovery in 1990 near Mt. Kirkpatrick near the South Pole. A large, Early Jurassic theropod was collected in sub-zero weather. The specimen is still being prepared, but it has an enormous transverse crest on top of the head, and is unlike any theropod ever found before.

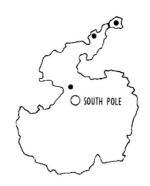

During Early Cretaceous times, both Antarctica and Australia were close to the South Pole. Nevertheless, dinosaur remains have been found on both continents.

The first dinosaur fossils recorded may be from China. Around AD 300, a Chinese scribe named Chang Qu wrote about the discovery of dragon bones near Wucheng in Sichuan province. Dinosaur bones are still found in that region, and there can be little doubt that in this case the words dragon and dinosaur are synonymous.

Left ~ In northern Africa, Ouranosaurus had to not only watch out for attacks by theropods like Spinosaurus, but it also had to be careful of the rivers and lakes where gigantic crocodiles like Sarcosuchus lay in wait of unwary prey.

The scientific discovery of dinosaurs in China came much later. The American Museum of Natural History expedition found dinosaur bones at Iren Dabasu (the Shining Lake) in 1921. This was the first major dinosaur site discovered there, and it still produces hundreds of dinosaur bones and eggs for each expedition that goes there. In 1922, hadrosaur bones were collected by Russian palaeontologists on the Amur River in Heilongjiang (at that time called Manchuria, hence the name of the dinosaur is *Mandschurosaurus*). Swedish palaeontologists recovered the remains of the sauropod *Euhelopus* from the eastern province of Shandong, and the specimens they collected can be seen today in Uppsala and Beijing.

China has a fantastic record of the history of dinosaurs, because virtually every time period of the Mesozoic is represented by terrestrial rocks. The dinosaurs recovered there are often the representatives of evolutionary steps not yet discovered anywhere else in the world. Although foreign expeditions worked in China for a long time, it has only been in the last 20 years that the Chinese have developed a significant interest in their own resources. The largest dinosaur museum in the world, and one of the most spectacular, was built over a gigantic bonebed of sauropods near Zigong in Sichuan Province. Most of the specimens are *Shunosaurus*, although another sauropod, the long-necked *Omeisaurus*, is found in the same quarry. Both of these animals had small clubs of bone on the ends of their whip-like tails. This region has also produced the greatest variety of stegosaurs known. Other dinosaur museums have opened in Erenhot (Inner Mongolia), Lufeng (Yunnan) and Zhucheng (Shandong), and most large cities have dinosaurs on display in their museums.

Numerous finds have been made in recent years in Yunnan province. In the Lufeng basin, local farmers collect dinosaur bones found when they terrace the hills for rice paddies, and use them for the construction of fences and sheds. Prosauropods are the most common specimens recovered from these brick red, Lower Jurassic sediments. One specimen was found south of Kunming together with a giant carnivore, and there was some speculation about the pair having died together in combat. However, there is no convincing evidence to support this story. The carnivore is extremely interesting, however, because it represents the first remains of the double-crested *Dilophosaurus* found outside of the United States, and is the only complete skeleton known.

Shantungosaurus remains from Shandong represent the largest hadrosaurs recovered anywhere. The specimens are usually found in the fields of farmers, which makes their discovery and collection rather unique. Road construction in Tibet uncovered dinosaurs at an altitude of 4,200 metres, higher than they have ever been discovered anywhere else. The high elevation was the result of mountain building activities after those dinosaurs perished, and they would have actually lived close to sea level.

Dinosaur remains are now known from 90% of the provinces and autonomous regions of China.

Dinosaur bones may have provided the inspiration for the mythical dragons of many cultures. Most of the dragon bones ground up for medicinal purposes in Asia are from more recent fossil mammals, however.

Right ~ Awkwardly raising itself on its hind limbs, Breviceratops reaches for some tender leaves. Evidence suggests that Late Cretaceous protoceratopsians from Mongolia were gregarious animals.

The Gobi Desert spans the border between China and Mongolia, and is one of the richest dinosaur collecting sites. As previously mentioned, it was opened up by the Third Asiatic Expedition of the American Museum of Natural History, from 1921 to 1930. Although its focus was much broader than palaeontology, they are most famous for their discoveries of dinosaur bones and eggs. The Sino-Swedish expeditions (1927-1935) found dinosaurs in Inner Mongolia, Gansu and Xinjiang, although not in the volumes recovered by the Americans. Russian expeditions into Mongolia in 1946, 1948 and 1949 measured their success in the tonnage of specimens collected. Amongst the prizes were full skeletons of *Tarbosaurus* and *Saurolophus*. The Sino-Soviet expeditions of 1959 and 1960 showed great promise for opening up dinosaur sites in northern China, but were terminated by political tensions between Moscow and Beijing. The Russians returned to the region in 1969–1970 as part of a collaborative effort with the Mongolian Academy of Sciences, and collected dinosaurs annually for twenty years. The latter expeditions were stimulated by the highly successful Polish-Mongolian expeditions (1963-1971) led by Zofia Kielan-Jaworowska. The quality of material collected was astounding, and many new taxa were described. Expedition members included Rinchen Barsbold and Altangerl Perle, two Mongolians who have since become well-known internationally as dinosaur collectors and research scientists. From 1986 to 1990, Canadian and Chinese scientists continued the tradition of large multinational and multidisciplinary expeditions to central Asia. More than a dozen new types of dinosaurs were discovered, and it will be many years before all the specimens are prepared and studied. In the meantime, an exhibition of the most significant specimens is travelling internationally as Dinosaur World Tour - the Greatest Show Un-earthed. Other Gobi expeditions include Japanese, American, French, Italian and others.

Shantungosaurus was one of the enormous hadrosaurs from the Late Cretaceous of Asia.

India once formed part of Gondwanaland, and it was only late in the Mesozoic that it pulled away and drifted north. As it slammed into Asia after the end of the Cretaceous, the Himalayas and other mountain chains were pushed up in the region of contact. So although India is now located in the northern hemisphere, most of its dinosaurs are characteristic of the southern hemisphere.

Barapasaurus, discovered in 1960, is one of the most primitive sauropods known, and is an intriguing glimpse into the character of Early Jurassic faunas. Upper Jurassic strata have produced dinosaurs, but the best known finds are probably from Upper Cretaceous rocks. Dinosaur fossils were recovered from these beds as early as 1860, and in the 1920s they produced the large theropod *Indosuchus*, titanosaurid sauropods and the supposed stegosaur *Dravidosaurus*.

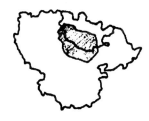

The Gobi is one of the great deserts of the world, stretching 2,000 kilometres along the border between China and Mongolia. Within the desert are many exposures of dinosaur bearing rocks that produce a treasure-trove of skeletons, eggs and nests.

There are many problems with the Indian Mesozoic fossil record that need to be addressed. Some of the dinosaurs suggest that India could not have been an island continent during the Jurassic because almost identical sauropods are found in South America and India. Other later forms are interesting because they show strong similarities to forms found in southern China, suggesting that the Asiatic contact may have occurred earlier than generally believed.

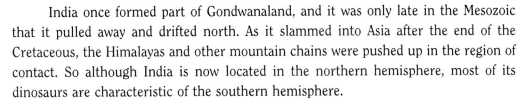

Left ~ With the passing of the storm, the Kritosaurus resumes browsing along the river bank. Like most large herbivores, it probably spent most of its waking hours eating, and may have consumed several hundred kilograms of leaves and twigs daily.

Dinosaurs are rare in Australia, although more intensive investigation in recent years has increased the numbers of places where they are found.

Relatively few dinosaurs have been recovered from Australia, and most are from Lower Cretaceous beds of Victoria and Queensland. Few palaeontologists have worked as hard as Tom and Pat Rich to collect specimens. On the shores of Dinosaur Cove, tunnels were dug into the hard rocks of a sea cliff. Sometimes working for weeks on end without seeing more than a few scraps of dinosaur bone, their persistence has nevertheless paid off with small and large theropods, and a bewildering assortment of hypsilophodonts. The peculiar fauna can be explained by examination of the palaeogeographic position of Australia during the Early Cretaceous. Situated well within the Antarctic Circle, the dinosaurs recovered by the Rich team were relatively small forms that had to eke out an existence during the sunless winter months when temperatures often fell below freezing point. Not surprisingly, some of these small dinosaurs had enormous eyes for seeing in the dark.

Other Australian finds include a wonderful trackway site near Winton documenting a herd of small dinosaurs being stampeded by a larger meat-eater. *Muttaburrasaurus* is an iguanodontid, and one of the largest dinosaurs found on that continent. The

Life abounded on the deltas and flood plains of North America during the Late Cretaceous. For the most part, the dinosaurs coexisted peacefully with each other, and ignored the activities of turtles, lizards, crocodiles, pterosaurs, birds and mammals. They were well

diminutive *Minmi* is a small but mature ankylosaur found in Queensland. Other footprint sites have been found in recent years in Western Australia.

Since the first discovery of dinosaur bones in England in 1822, the search for the bones of the great saurians has been going on all over Europe. Dinosaur fossils have been discovered in most countries, and new specimens are being recovered all the time. The *Iguanodon* discoveries of Belgium, the rich *Plateosaurus* bonebeds of Germany, and the eggs and nests of southern France have already been mentioned. All good specimens of the link between dinosaurs and birds, *Archaeopteryx*, were recovered from the lithographic limestones of Solnhofen.

The discovery of *Baryonyx*, a large, long-snouted theropod, from Surrey in England, is one of the more spectacular discoveries in recent years. Austria and Switzerland have produced dinosaur fossils, but dinosaur hunting has been more intensive on the Isle of Wight, in southern France, Spain, Portugal, and Romania. The southern European dinosaurs show a mixture of Asian, North American and African influences that presents intriguing problems.

adapted to their environments, so there was no reason to suspect that extinction was imminent. But a few million years later, only the birds remained as testament to the success of the dinosaurs.

WHERE CAN YOU SEE DINOSAURS?

Museums in which Dinosaurs Can be Seen

Argentina

Buenos Aires: Argentine Museum of Natural Sciences
La Plata: Museum of La Plata University
San Miguel de Tucumán: Museum of Natural Sciences

Australia

Adelaide, South Australia: South Australian Museum
Fortitude Valley, Queensland: Queensland Museum
Melbourne: Museum of Victoria
Perth, Western Australia: Western Australian Museum
Sydney, New South Wales: Australian Museum

Austria

Vienna: Natural History Museum

Belgium

Bernissart, Hainaut: Bernissart Museum
Brussels: Royal Institute of Natural Sciences

Brazil

Rio de Janeiro: National Museum

Canada

Calgary, Alberta: Calgary Zoo & Prehistoric Park
Drumheller, Alberta: Royal Tyrrell Museum of Palaeontology
Edmonton, Alberta: Provincial Museum of Alberta
Ottawa, Ontario: Canadian Museum of Nature
Quebec: Redpath Museum
Toronto, Ontario: Royal Ontario Museum
Vancouver, British Columbia: University of British Columbia, Geology Museum

China

Beijing (Peking): Beijing Natural History Museum
Beijing (Peking): Institute of Vertebrate Palaeontology and Palaeoanthropology
Beipei, Sichuan: Beipei Museum
Chengdu, Sichuan: College of Geology, Museum of Chengdu
Erenhot, Inner Mongolia: Erenhot Dinosaur Museum
Harbin: Heilongjiang Museum
Hohhot, Inner Mongolia: Inner Mongolia Museum
Lufeng, Yunnan: Lufeng Dinosaur Museum
Tianjin: Tianjin Museum of Natural History
Zhucheng, Shandong: Zhucheng Dinosaur Museum
Zigong, Sichuan: Zigong Dinosaur Museum

France

Aix-en-Provence: Natural History Museum
Le Havre: Natural History Museum
Nancy: Museum of Earth Sciences
Nantes: Natural History Museum
Paris: National Museum of Natural History

Germany

Berlin: Humboldt University, Natural History Museum
Eichstatt: Jura Museum, Willibaldsburg
Frankfurt am Main: Senckenberg Natural History Museum
Munich: Bavarian State Institute for Palaeontology and Historical Geology
Münster: Geological and Palaeontological Museum
Stuttgart: State Museum for Natural History
Tübingen: Institute and Museum for Geology and Palaeontology

India

Calcutta: Indian Statistical Institute, Geology Museum

Italy

Bologna: G. Capellini Museum
Milan: Museum of Natural History
Venice: Civic Museum of Natural History

Japan

Fukui: Fukui Prefecture Museum
Iwaki, Fukushima: Iwaki City Museum of Coal and Fossils
Kagoshima, Kagoshima: Kagoshima Prefectural Museum
Kitakyushu, Fukuoka: Kitakyushu Museum of Natural History
Kyoto: Kyoto Municipal Science Centre for Youth
Maebashi, Gunma: Gunma Prefectural Museum of History
Niigata, Niigata: Niigata Prefectural Natural Science Museum
Osaka: Osaka Museum of Natural History
Sapporo, Hokkaido: Historical Museum of Hokkaido
Sendai, Miyagi: Saito Ho-on Kai Museum of Natural History
Shimizu, Shizuoka: Tokai University, Natural History Museum
Takikawa, Hokkaido: Takikawa Museum of Art and Natural History
Tokyo: National Science Museum
Toyohashi, Aichi: Toyohashi Museum of Natural History
Utsunomiya, Tochigi: Tochigi Prefecture Museum

Mexico

Mexico City: Natural History Museum

Mongolia

Ulan-Bator: State Central Museum

Morocco

Rabat: Museum of Earth Sciences

Niger

Niamey: National Museum

Norway

Oslo: Museum of Palaeontology

Poland

Chorzów: Dinosaur Valley, Silesian Zoo
Warsaw: State Museum
Warsaw: Museum of Evolution, Polish Academy of Sciences

Russia

Moscow: Orlov Palaeontological Museum
St. Petersburg: Central Geological and Prospecting Museum

South Africa

Cape Town: South Africa Museum
Johannesburg: Bernard Price Institute of Palaeontology

Spain

Madrid: National Museum of Natural Science

Sweden

Stockholm: Swedish Museum of Natural History
Uppsala: Uppsala University, Palaeontological Museum

Switzerland

Geneva: Natural History Museum

United Kingdom

Birmingham: Birmingham Museum
Cambridge: Cambridge University, Sedgwick Museum
Dorchester: Dorchester Museum
Edinburgh: Royal Scottish Museum
Elgin, Scotland: Elgin Museum
Glasgow, Scotland: Hunterian Museum
Ipswich, Suffolk : Ipswich Museum
London: Museum of Natural History
London: Crystal Palace Park
Oxford: University Museum
Sandown, Isle of Wight: Museum of Isle of Wight Geology

United States of America

Amherst, Massachusetts: Amherst College Museum
Ann Arbor, Michigan: University of Michigan, Museum of Palaeontology
Austin, Texas: Texas Memorial Museum
Berkeley, California: University of California, Museum of Palaeontology
Boulder, Colorado: University of Colorado, Natural History Museum
Bozeman, Montana: Museum of the Rockies
Buffalo, New York: Buffalo Museum of Science
Cambridge, Massachusetts: Harvard University, Museum of Comparative Zoology
Chicago, Illinois: Field Museum of Natural History
Cincinnati, Ohio: Cincinnati Museum of Natural History
Cleveland, Ohio: Cleveland Museum of Natural History
Denver, Colorado: Denver Museum of Natural History
Fairbanks, Alaska: University of Alaska, Museum
Flagstaff, Arizona: Museum of Northern Arizona
Fort Worth, Texas: Fort Worth Museum of Science
Hays, Kansas: Sternberg Memorial Museum
Houston, Texas: Houston Museum of Natural Sciences
Laramie, Wyoming: University of Wyoming, W. H. Reed Museum
Lawrence, Kansas: University of Kansas, Museum of Natural History
Lincoln, Nebraska: University of Nebraska, State Museum
Los Angeles, California: Los Angeles County Museum of Natural History
Milwaukee, Wisconsin: Milwaukee Public Museum
New Haven, Connecticut: Yale University, Peabody Museum of Natural History
New York City, New York: American Museum of Natural History
Norman, Oklahoma: University of Oklahoma, Stouall Museum
Philadelphia, Pennsylvania: Academy of Natural Sciences
Pittsburgh, Pennsylvania: Carnegie Museum of Natural History
Price, Utah: College of Eastern Utah, Prehistoric Museum
Provo, Utah: Brigham Young University, Earth Science Museum
St. Paul, Minnesota: The Science Museum of Minnesota
Salt Lake City, Utah: Utah Museum of Natural History
San Francisco, California: California Academy of Science
Vernal, Utah: Utah Natural History State Museum
Washington, D.C.: National Museum of Natural History, Smithsonian Institution

Zimbabwe

Harare: National Museum of Zimbabwe

Dinosaur Parks

Cleveland-Lloyd Quarry, south of Price, Utah, is where hundreds of bones of *Allosaurus* have been excavated from a bonebed. Many of these bones were used to make composite skeletons of *Allosaurus* that can be seen in museums worldwide.

Dinosaur National Monument, near Vernal, Utah, is best known for its visitor centre, which is built over a partially excavated bonebed. Many of the most famous dinosaurs can be seen in the cliff face, including skeletons of *Allosaurus*, *Apatosaurus*, *Camarasaurus*, and *Stegosaurus*.

Dinosaur Provincial Park, near Brooks (Alberta, Canada), is a UNESCO World Heritage Site. Stretched along the Red Deer River, the badlands have been one of the most productive sites for dinosaur skeletons. In addition to 35 species of dinosaurs, more than 75 species of fish, turtles, lizards, crocodiles, pterosaurs, birds and mammals have been found in the Upper Cretaceous rocks. More than 300 skeletons have been excavated from the Park, and have found their way into 35 museums.

The Dinosaur Triangle is not a park, but it is becoming a well-known route connecting some of the most famous dinosaur sites in Utah and Colorado, including Cleveland-Lloyd, Dinosaur Hill, Dinosaur National Monument, Dry Mesa Quarry, Fruita Palaeontological Area, Rabbit Valley Palaeontological Area, Rigg's Hill, some great footprint and bone sites near Moab, and much more.

Egg Mountain, near Choteau (Montana), is a beautiful stretch of badlands within sight of the front ranges of the Rocky Mountains. Dinosaur eggs and embryos, and an immense bonebed composed almost entirely of *Maiasaura* are some of the palaeontological riches.

Ghost Ranch, New Mexico, is the home of *Coelophysis*. The quarry that has produced hundreds of skeletons can be visited, although little can be seen at this time. The visitor centre has some excellent displays, including a slab of rock from the quarry that is being prepared in public.

Petrified Forest, Arizona, is most famous for its agatized tree trunks, but has also produced one of the earliest records of dinosaurs (a staurikosaur), *Coelophysis*, and dinosaur footprints.

Rocky Hill Dinosaur State Park, Connecticut, has a huge building constructed over part of a Lower Jurassic dinosaur footprint site. Hundreds of footprints are visible, most of which are in trackways.

Winton in Queensland (Australia) protects a dinosaur footprint site where hundreds of footprints tell a dramatic story. A group of small dinosaurs, when approached by a large theropod, turned and fled, leaving the record of the encounter in the mud.

Volunteer Programmes

There are many museums that operate dinosaur collecting programmes during the summer months with the assistance of volunteers. Most museums charge per diem rates to help defray the expense of food and lodging, and in other cases a set rate is charged for a predetermined period of time. This is money well spent, and generally is much cheaper than taking a regular vacation. Most large museums will also accept studious volunteers to help prepare fossils, curate collections, and a variety of other tasks. The listing below is not complete, and if you are interested in working on dinosaurs, write to the museum of your choice to see if they can accommodate you.

Dinamation Society (Fruita, Colorado) operate a number of dinosaur quarries in the United States and Mexico using people who are willing to assist in funding the excavations.

Earthwatch is an organization that charges people to assist on expeditions around the world. They offer a variety of programs, not just for collecting dinosaurs. The Dinosaur Cove excavation in Australia is one of the many programmes that has been offered in the past.

The Milwaukee Public Museum has run their Dinosaur Dash programme for more than 10 years. The fieldwork is done in the Upper Cretaceous badlands of Eastern Utah.

The Museum of the Rockies (Bozeman, Montana) has one of the largest dinosaur excavation programmes, and use volunteers at Egg Mountain and other sites.

The Royal Tyrrell Museum of Palaeontology (Drumheller, Alberta, Canada) has been using volunteers in dinosaur digs since 1978, and has taken on hundreds of volunteers from Australia, Austria, Britain, Canada, China, Denmark, France, Germany, Nepal, Sweden, and the United States. Most volunteers work in Dinosaur Provincial Park or Devil's Coulee Egg Site. There are a limited number of positions each year, and volunteers are required to commit to 3 weeks or more. A smaller, cost recovery program is operated in Drumheller.

New Discoveries

The authors have attempted to include in the text the most up to date information on significant dinosaur discoveries. Many of these have not yet been scientifically described, a process that can take many years of preparation and study.

New dinosaur discoveries are being made every few months in some part of the world. Sometimes the discoveries are made in the field, and sometimes in museum cabinets.

At present, the most intensively worked field sites for dinosaurs are in Argentina, western Canada, China, Mongolia and the western United States. A lot of interest has been developing in Africa in recent years, because this is an area where our knowledge of dinosaurs is deficient. There is great potential for major dinosaur discoveries in the polar regions. Americans, Canadians, Danes and

Russians have been searching in the Arctic, while Argentine, American and British scientists have achieved similar successes in Antarctica.

In spite of public and scientific interest in dinosaurs, we know relatively little about these magnificent animals. Even intensively collected sites continue to produce new types of dinosaurs and new information. Dinosaurs are not always found in badlands and deserts, either. The discovery of *Baryonyx* in Surrey (England) and *Tyrannosaurus* in a building excavation in Denver (U.S.A.) are just two examples of significant specimens turning up in unexpected places. As long as the rocks are the right age, and represent the right kinds of depositional environments, the possibility always exists of finding dinosaur bones because they lived on every continent in virtually every land-based environment that was available to them.

Dinosaur Experts Active Today

The following names are those of the most active dinosaur researchers in the world today. The list is not exhaustive, and there are more than thirty people regularly publishing scientific papers on dinosaurs. Even so, this is a relatively low number of experts to cover the geographic (worldwide) and temporal (150 million years) range of such successful animals.

Dr. Robert T. Bakker (Boulder, Colorado) is most famous for presenting evidence in favour of warm-blooded dinosaurs. In addition to developing and championing some of the most innovative research on dinosaurs, he has done excellent anatomical studies of theropods.

Dr. José Bonaparte (Buenos Aires) is responsible for the proliferation of interest in the dinosaurs of Argentina. He was involved in the description of the bizarre theropod *Carnotaurus*.

Dr. Philip J. Currie (Royal Tyrrell Museum of Palaeontology, Drumheller) has the enviable position of being situated in the badlands of Alberta. Theropods, the origin of birds and dinosaur migrating behaviour are his greatest research interests, but he works on ankylosaurs, ceratopsians, hadrosaurs and pterosaurs when he finds time.

Dr. Peter Dodson (School of Veterinary Medicine, University of Pennsylvania, Philadelphia) has produced some of the most thought-provoking papers on growth and variation in dinosaurs, palaeoecology, and ceratopsians.

Dong Zhiming (Institute of Vertebrate Palaeontology and Palaeoanthropology, Academy of Sciences, Beijing) has probably been involved in the collection and description of more dinosaurs than anyone alive today.

Dr. John (Jack) Horner (Museum of the Rockies, Bozeman, Montana) is the foremost expert on duckbilled dinosaurs, and has done excellent work associated with the eggs, babies, histology, parental behaviour and evolution of these animals.

Dr. Martin Lockley (University of Colorado, Denver) has become the leading expert on dinosaur footprints and trackways. He has worked extensively in the United States and Korea, and has published several books on the subject.

Dr. John Ostrom (Yale University) has worked on every major group of dinosaurs during the course of his long and very productive career. He is best remembered, however, for the discovery and description of *Deinonychus*. By this action, he triggered the Dinosaur Renaissance that started in the 1970s and is still growing today.

Dr. Dale Russell (Canadian Museum of Nature, Ottawa) is most famous for his papers on palaeoecology, ornithomimids, tyrannosaurids, and the evolution of intelligence. He has collected dinosaurs worldwide, but probably attracted the most attention for his role in the Canada-China Dinosaur Project.

Dr. Paul Sereno (University of Chicago) has collected dinosaurs in Argentina, Niger and the United States, and has studied specimens worldwide. He is most famous for the discovery of *Eoraptor* and *Herrerasaurus*, and for his research on dinosaur origins.

CONCLUSION

Dinosaurs ruled the world for more than 150 million years. They represent a line of archosaurs that adapted rapidly to changing palaeoclimatic and palaeogeographic conditions. Late Triassic carnivorous dinosaurs diversified speedily into carnivorous and herbivorous forms, and attained giant dimensions with bizarre, awe-inspiring forms. They also produced small, lightly built, fast, feather-covered types that opened the era of flying dinosaurs – the Age of Birds. This lineage survived whatever killed off the rest of the dinosaurs at the end of the Cretaceous, and all of the subsequent upheavals, changes and catastrophes of the Tertiary and the Ice Ages to produce more than 8,000 living species. Consequently, dinosaurs have not died out. They are alive and well, and perhaps will even survive the Era of Man.

Index

Abdominal ribs 20
Abelisauridae 68, 96
Acanthopholis 126
Accessory hearts in the neck 52
Acrocanthosaurus 68, 69, 90, 91, 93
Adaptation 142
Adaptation of archosaurs 20
Adasaurus 102
Aegyptosaurus 86
Aepisaurus 86
Air sacs 44
Alamosaurus 86, 87
Albertosaurus 82, 87, 91, 103, 142, 152
Alectrosaurus 87, 93, 103
Algae 38
Algoasaurus 86
Alioramus 93
Alligatorellus 42
Alligatorium 42
Allosauridae 68
Allosaurus 12, 34, 35, 63, 67–69, 76, 172
Altispinax 96
Alvarez, L. W. 159
Alxasaurus 98
Amargasaurus 58, 59
Amargasaurus cazaui 52
Ameghino, Carlos 163
Ameghino, Florentino 163
Ammonites 25, 39, 43
Ammonites extinction 159
Ammosaurus 39
Amtosaurus 127
Anatotitan 115
Anchiceratops 130, 133, 137
Anchisaurids 37
Anchisaurus 39
Andrews, Roy Chapman 14, 150/151
Angiosperms 80, 83
Ankylosauria 73, 125–127
Ankylosauridae 73, 125,
Ankylosaurs 16, 106, 125–129
Ankylosaurus 93, 126, 127
Anomodontia 26
Anserimimus 99
Antarctosaurus 86
Antorbital window 20
Apatosaurus 12, 33, 39, 48, 49, 172
Aralosaurus 115
Archaeopteryx 17, 169
Archaeornithomimus 99
Archetypes 25
Archosauria 15, 20
Arrhinoceratops 130, 133, 137, 159
Asiaceratops 134
Asiatosaurus 60
Aspidorhynchus 17
Astragalus 17
Astrodon 87
Atlascopcosaurus 107
Avaceratops 132

Bactrosaurus 115
Bagaceratops 134
Bakker, Robert T. 15, 43, 49, 142, 174
Barapasaurus 44, 48, 167
Barsbold, Rinchen 167
Barsboldia 115, 118
Baryonyx 79, 169, 173
Bayn Dzak 14, 134, 151
Behavioural adaptations 147
Bellosaurus 76
Bennettitales 25, 38
Bergmann's rule 37
Bernissart 13, 108
Big Dinosaur Quarry 12
Bird-hipped dinosaurs 16
Bird hips 17
Birds 13, 15, 28, 33, 34
Birds, flightless 100
Bonaparte, José 163, 174
Bone Cabin Quarry 12, 48
Bonebeds 115
Brachiosauridae 58
Brachiosaurs 45

Brachiosaurus 33, 48, 86, 142, 162
Brachiosaurus altithorax 58
Brachiosaurus brancai 58
Brachyceratops 132
Brachylophosaurus 112, 115, 137
Bradycneme 101
Brain 16
Brain of sauropods 43
Breviceratops 130, 134, 164
"*Brontosaurus*" 48
Broom, Robert 162
Brown, Barnum 13
Buckland, William 11

Caenagnathus 103
Calamospondylus 69
Camarasauridae 48
Camarasaurids 60, 86
Camarasaurus 12, 45, 48, 52, 60, 172
Camptosauridae 108
Camptosaurus 12, 39
Cannibalistic behaviour 34
Carcharodontosaurus 90
Carnegie, Andrew 49
Carnosauria 60, 63, 90
Carnosaurs 34, 60, 69, 90
Carnotaurus 5, 34, 68, 96, 97
Catastrophe, natural 152
Catastrophic destruction of dinosaurs 159
Caytoniales 38
Centrosaurinae 130, 134
Centrosaurine ceratopsids 132, 137
Centrosaurines 130
Centrosaurus 34, 130, 132, 137, 138, 141, 146, 147, 148
Centrosaurus, bonebed 148
Ceratopsia 16, 127, 130
Ceratopsians 16, 106
Ceratopsidae 130, 134, 137
Ceratopsids 134, 137
Ceratosauridae 63
Ceratosaurus 12, 34, 62, 67, 68
Cetiosauridae 48
Cetiosaurus 44, 52
Chang Qu 163
Charig, Alan 162
Chasmosaurinae 130, 134
Chasmosaurine ceratopsids 133
Chasmosaurus 133–135, 137, 138
Chatterjee, Sankar 99
Cheek bone (jugal) 130
Chiayusaurus 60
Chubutisaurus 87
Chungkingosaurus 77
Claosaurus 115
Clathropteris 38
Cleveland-Lloyd Quarry 172
Coelacanths 84
Coelophysis 34, 35, 63, 172
Coelurosauridae 72
Coelurosaurs 34
Coloradisaurus 39
Comodactylus 52, 60
Compsognathus 17
Conchoraptor 103
Conifers 81
Cope, Edward Drinker 12, 13
Cope's Quarry 12
Corythosaurus 112, 115, 118, 156
Cranial nerves 156
Craterosaurus 124
Crest of lambeosaurine hadrosaurs 112
Crest of *Parasaurolophus* 160
Crests 63
Crocodiles 21
Crocodilians 39
Crompton, A. W. 162
Currie, Philip J. 174
Cuvier, Georges 11
Cycadeoidales 25
Cycadophytes 25
Cycads 79, 83
Cypresses 25

Dacentrurus 77

Darwin, Charles 12
Daspletosaurus 91
Dasycladaceae 38
Dead Lodge Canyon 13
Deinocheiridae 99
Deinocheirus 99
Deinonychus 87, 101, 102, 108, 109, 142
Denversaurus 126
Devil's Coulee 152
Diapsida 20
Dicraeosaurus 49, 52, 162
Dilophosaurus 34, 42, 63, 72, 164
Dinamation Society (Fruita Colorado) 173
Dinosaur bones in Palaeocene beds 154
Dinosaur brain 152, 156
Dinosaur Cove 168
Dinosaur expeditions 162
Dinosaur experts active today 174
Dinosaur extinction theories 161
Dinosaur footprints in Korea 156
Dinosaur National Monument 12, 101, 172
Dinosaur origins 174
Dinosaur Provincial Park 13, 106, 146, 147, 154, 172
Dinosaur Triangle 172
Dinosauria 10, 11, 15
Dinosauroid 160
Dinosaurs' ancestors 20
Dinosaurs' diversification 33
Dinosaurs – history of discovery 10
Dinosaurs in the Jurassic 42
Dinosaurs – the first 28
Diplodocidae 48
Diplodocids 48, 49, 87
Diplodocus 12, 33, 43, 45, 48
Diplodocus carnegii 49
Dipteridaceae 38
Discoglossus 39
Dodson, Peter 15, 174
Dollo, Louis 13
Dravidosaurus 124, 167
Dromaeosauridae 100
Dromaeosaurids 34, 102, 152
Dromaeosaurs 21, 137
Dromaeosaurus 34, 87, 101, 102
Dromiceiomimus 99
Dry Mesa Quarry 67
Dryptosaurus 93

Earthwatch 173
Edmontonia 16, 125, 126
Edmontosaurus 112, 115, 118, 147
Egg-laying animals 49
Egg Mountain 172
Eggs and nests 149
Elaphrosaurus 99
Elasmosaurus 39
Elmisaurids 34, 103
Environment 154
Eoceratops 154
Eoraptor 26, 29, 32, 33, 37, 163, 174
Equisetites munsteri 38
Erenhot 164
Erlikosaurus 96, 98
Euhelopus 49, 60, 164
Euoplocephalus 127, 129
Euskelosaurus 162
Eustreptospondylus 62, 68, 69
Excrement, coprolites 156

Farlow, Jim 15
Flaming Cliffs 14, 151, 154
Flying dinosaurs 174
Flying reptiles 22
Footprint sites 115
Frills of ceratopsians 138
Frogs 12, 13, 39, 84, 156

Gallimimus 99, 100
Galton, Peter 15
Gansu 167
Garudimimus 99
Gasparini, Zulmo 163
Gastroliths 45, 52

Geosaurus 39
Germanodactylus 69
Gertie 32
Ghost Ranch 34, 35, 172
Gilette, David 49, 52
Gilmoreosaurus 115
Ginkgo 25, 38, 79, 83
Gleicheniaceae 25
Gobi Desert 167
Gobisaurus 127
Golden Age of dinosaurs 78
Gondwanaland 38, 43
Goyocephale 124
Gradualist Theory of Extinction 159
Gravitholus 124
Great Extinction 159
Growth rings 145
Gryposaurus 115, 156
Gymnosperms 25

Hadrosaur eggs 149
Hadrosaurines 112
Hadrosaurs 86, 107, 109, 112, 115, 124
Hadrosaurus 115
Haeckel, Ernst 12
Halticosaurus 34
Haplocanthosaurus 48
Harpymimus 99
Herrerasaurus 28, 29, 32, 33, 163, 174
Histology of dinosaur bones 145
Homalocephale 120, 124
Hoplitosaurus 126
Horned dinosaurs 127
Horner, John (Jack) 149, 151, 174
Horsetails 25
Huayangosaurus 73, 77
Huene, Friedrich von 14, 22, 35, 37, 93, 163
Huxley, Thomas Henry 12
Hylaeosaurus 69, 126
Hypacrosaurus 115, 116, 118, 152
Hypacrosaurus altispinus 118
Hypselosaurus 86, 149
Hypselosaurus priscus 149
Hypsilophodon 106–108, 163
Hypsilophodontidae 107
Hypsilophodonts in Australia 106, 168

Ichthyosaurs 39
Iguanodon 11, 13, 107–109, 147
Iguanodon bernissartensis 109
Iguanodontidae 108, 109
Indosuchus 93, 167
Indricotherium 144
Ingenia 103
Inoceramus 84
Iren Dabasu 164
Ischisaurus 33

Janensch, Werner 162
Jaxartosaurus 115, 118
Jurassic 38 ff.

Kentrosaurus 62, 77, 162
Kielan Jaworowska, Zofia 167
Kowalevski, Vladimir O. 12
Kritosaurus 167
Kunming 164

La Brea tar pits 69
Lagosuchus 26
Lambeosaurines 112
Lambeosaurus 112, 115, 118
Laparrent, Albert de 162
Laurasia 38, 43
Leakey, Louis 162
Lealellynasaura 107
Leptoceratops 130, 134
Lesotho 162
Lesothosaurus 32, 33
Lewes 10, 11
Liliensternus 34
Lizard-hipped dinosaurs 16
Lizard hips 17
Lockley, Martin 174

Lophorhothon 115
Lufeng basin 164
Lufeng (Yunnan) 164
Lufengosaurus 39
Lusitanosaurus 73

Macrocephalosaurus 102
Macrodontophion 68
Maiasaura 115, 118, 147, 150–152, 172
Majungatholus 124
Makela, Bob 151
Maleevus 127
Mamenchisaurus 44, 55, 58, 60, 145
Mammal-like reptiles 26
Mammals 13, 25, 26
Manchuria 164
Mandschurosaurus 115, 118, 164
Mantell, Gideon 10, 11
Mantell, Mary Ann 10, 11, 13
Marsh, Othniel Charles 12, 107
Marsh's Quarry 12
Marsupials 82, 84
Massospondylids 37
Massospondylus 39, 42, 43, 162
Matheron, Philippe 149
Mating of dinosaurs 151
Matoniaceae 38
Megalosauridae 67
Megalosaurus 11, 34, 67–69, 90, 96
Metriorhynchus 39
Microceratops 134
Micropachycephalosaurus 124
Microscopic structure of the bones 150
Microvertebrate sites 84
Migration of dinosaurs 148
Minmi 125, 126, 169
Monoclonius 12, 132, 137
Monolophosaurus 67, 68, 69
Mononykus 28
Montanoceratops 134, 144
Morrison Formation 12
Mosasaurs 84
Museum, American, of Natural History 12, 14, 167
Museum, British (Natural History) 163
Museum La Plata 163
Museum, Milwaukee Public 175
Museum of the Rockies (Bozeman) 149, 173
Museum, Royal, in Brussels 13
Museum, Royal Tyrrell, of Palaeontology 173
Museum, Senckenberg, of Natural History 112
Museums in which dinosaurs can be seen 170, 171
Mussaurus 38, 39
Muttaburrasaurus 109, 168
Muttaburrasaurus langdoni 109

Nanotyrannus 91
Nanshiungosaurus 98
Nautilus 43
Nemegt Valley 141
Nemegtosaurus 58, 87
Nest 128
Nests of hadrosaurs 115
Nests of Maiasaura 152
New discoveries 173
Nipponosaurus 115, 118
Nodosaurid 126
Nodosaurid ankylosaurs 126, 127
Nodosauridae 73, 125
Nodosaurids 125, 127
Nodosaurus 12, 126
Nopcsa 73
Notobatrachus 39

Omeisaurus 48, 60, 164
Omeisaurus jungschiensis 60
Opisthocoelicaudia 60, 87
Opossum 82
Ornatotholus 124
Ornithischia 12, 32, 103, 106
Ornithischian dinosaurs 33, 38
Ornithischian forms 14
Ornithischians 103, 106
Ornithomimidae 99
Ornithomimids 99, 152
Ornithomimus 12, 34, 87, 99
Ornithopoda 106

Ornithosuchia 26
Ornithosuchidae 26
Orodromeus 107, 108
Orodromeus makeli 152
Osborn, Henry Fairfield 12, 14, 150
Ostrich mimics 99
Ostriches of dinosaur world 99
Ostrom, John 15, 174
Othnielia 107
Ouranosaurus 93, 109, 163
Oviraptor 87, 103
Oviraptorids 34
Owen, Richard 10, 11, 12

Pachycephalosauridae 118, 120, 121
Pachycephalosaurs 124
Pachycephalosaurus 121, 124, 125, 132
Pachyrhinosaurus 130, 137, 138
Palaeobatrachus 39
Pangaea 24, 37, 38
Panoplosaurus 124–127
Paranthodon 124
Parasaurolophus 112, 115, 118, 156, 160
Paraucaria 38
Parkinson, James 11
Parksosaurus 107
Patagonia 38
Peak of diversity of sauropods 45
Peipehsuchus 67
Pelorosaurus 58, 87
Pelvis structure 16
Pentoceratops 133, 137, 156
Perle, Altangerl 167
Petrified Forest 25, 32, 172
Phylloceratidae 39
Physiological adaptation 142
Piatnitzkysaurus 68, 69
Pinacosaurus 127, 128
Pisanosaurus 32, 33
Piveteausaurus 69
Placentals 84
Plateosaurus 14, 35, 37, 38, 147, 169
Plesiosaurs 39
Pleurocoelus 87
Plot, Robert 10
Podozamites 38
Poekilopleuron 68
Polacanthus 125, 126
Polish-Mongolian expeditions 167
Predatory dinosaurs 90
Predentary 32
Prenocephale 124
Primates 84
Probactrosaurus 109
Proboscis of sauropods 45
Prosaurolophus 115, 152
Prosauropoda 26, 35, 37, 39
Protoceratops 103, 130, 134, 151
Protoceratopsidae 130, 134
Protoceratopsids 130, 134
Psittacosauridae 130
Psittacosaurus 130
Pterosaurs 15, 21, 22
Pubic boot 29

Quetzalcoatlus 21, 22

Rays 39
Rebbachisaurus 58, 87
Red Deer River 13
Ribs 16
Rich, Tom and Pat 168
Ricqles, Armand de 145
Rioarribasaurus 35
Rocky Hill Dinosaur State Park 172
Rostral bone 130
Russell, Dale 93, 174
Russell, Loris 142
Russian expeditions to Mongolia 167

Saichania 127
Salamanders 156
Saltasaurus 86, 87
Sarcolestes 126, 127
Sarcosuchus 163
Saurischia 12, 32
Saurischian dinosaurs 16, 33, 38
Saurischian forms 14
Saurolophus 87, 102, 115, 118, 156, 167
Sauropelta 125, 126
Sauropoda 42–44, 86

Sauropodomorpha 25
Sauropodomorphs 26, 43
Sauropods 16, 26, 42–44, 60
Saurornithoides 101
Saurornitholestes 101, 102, 152
Scelidosaurus 73, 76
Scleromochlus 22
Scrotum humanum 10
Scutellosaurus 73
Secernosaurus 115
Secondary palate 21
Seeley, Harry Govier 12, 14
Segnosauridae 96
Segnosaurus 98, 99
Seguin, A. R. 160
Seismosaurus 43, 45, 52, 54, 55
Seismosaurus halli 49
Sellosaurus 39
Sereno, Paul 28, 163, 174
Serrations 62
Sexual variation 134
Shamosaurus 127
Shandong 164
Shantungosaurus 115, 118, 120, 164, 167
Sharks 39
Shunosaurus 48, 49, 164
Shuvosaurus 99
Siberia 24, 38
Sichuan Province 164
Silvisaurus 126
Sino-Canadian expeditions 54, 103, 127
Sino-Soviet expeditions 167
Sino-Swedish expeditions 167
Sinornithoides 101
Sinraptor 68, 69, 76
Skin impression 16
Slovakia 34
Solenopora 38
Spinosauridae 93, 96
Spinosaurus 90, 109, 163
Staurikosaur 172
Staurikosaurus 28, 29, 32, 33, 37, 163
Stegocephalians 25
Stegoceras 124
Stegosauria 72–77
Stegosaurs 69, 124
Stegosaurus 12, 172
Stegosaurus stenops 76, 77
Stenonychosaurus 160
Stenopelix 130
Sternberg, Charles H. 13
Stonesfield 11
Straelen, Victor van 149
Struthiomimus 99
"Struthiosaurus" 126
Stutchbury, Samuel 11
Stygimoloch 120, 122, 124
Styracosaurus 130, 132, 134, 137, 138
Supersaurus 52, 68
Syntarsus 32, 34, 63
Szechuanosaurus 68

Talarurus 127
Tail of sauropods 44
Tanius 115
Taquet, Philippe 162
Tarbosaurus 93, 167
Tarchia 126, 127
Taxodiaceae 38
Technosaurus 32, 33
Teeth of dinosaurs 16
Teeth of meat-eating dinosaurs (theropods) 62
Teeth of sauropods 43, 60
Telmatosaurus 115, 118
Temporal opening, lateral 20
Temporal opening, upper 20
Tendaguru (Tanzania) 162
Tenontosaurus 106, 108, 109
Termoregulation 142
Tethys Sea 24, 38
Thaumathopteris 38
Thecodont archosaur 26
Thecodonts 20, 26
Thecodontosaurids 37
Therapsids 26
Theriodontia 26
Therizinosaurus 98
Theropoda 34, 90
Theropods 26, 33, 34, 103
Thescelosaurus 107, 108, 138

Third Asiatic Expedition 14, 167
Thoracic region of a sauropod 44
Thulborn, Tony 26
Thyreophora 73
Thyreophorons 73, 76
Tienchisaurus 127
Tienshanosaurus 60
Titanosaurid sauropods 86, 167
Tornieria 86
Torosaurus 12, 127, 130, 133, 134, 136
Torvosaurus 60, 67, 68, 69
Trackway sites 45
Tree ferns 38
Trematosaurus 25
Triadobatrachus massinoti 25
Triassic 24 ff.
Triceratops 12, 130, 133, 134, 137, 138
Troodon 16, 34, 84, 87, 93, 152, 160
Troodontidae 101
Troodontids 34
Troodontids – the relatives of true birds 103
Trössingen 14
Tsintaosaurus 115, 118
Tuojiangosaurus 69, 77
Turanoceratops 132
Tylocephale 124
Tyrannosaur 112
Tyrannosauridae 91
Tyrannosaurids 28
Tyrannosaurus 12, 33, 34, 68, 87, 93, 103, 136, 173
Tyrannosaurus rex 91

Udanoceratops 130, 134
Ultrasauros 48, 58, 68
Ultrasauros mcintoshi 58, 60
Utahraptor 101, 102

Valdosaurus 108
Varanus griseus 43
Velociraptor 34, 87, 101
Ventral ribs 63
Vertebrae 16, 20
Vieraella 39
Volunteer programmes 172
Vulcanodon 44, 48

Wannanosaurus 124
Warm-blooded dinosaurs 15
Winton 168, 172
Wuerhosaurus 124

Xinjiang (China) 124, 167

Yandusaurus 107
Yangchuanosaurus 68, 69
Yaverlandia 124
Yews 25
Yunnan province 164
Yunnanosaurids 37

Zephyrosaurus 107
Zhiming, Dong 174
Zhucheng (Shandong) 164
Zigong 164
Zimbabwe 48